God's Creations

Eden Press

God's Creations

Edited by
Rebecca Mee

First published in Great Britain in 1998 by Poetry Today, an imprint of
Penhaligon Page Ltd, 12 Godric Square, Maxwell Road, Peterborough. PE2 7JJ

A Catalogue record for this book is available from the British Library

ISBN 1 86226 096 6

Typesetting and layout, Penhaligon Page Ltd, England
Printed and bound by Forward Press Ltd, England

Foreword

I have always felt that by expressing our thoughts, feelings and observations of life from a Christian standpoint, others could learn from them; I personally, can't think of a better way to express them than through the medium of poetry. Thus it is my hope that the collection of poetry in *God's Creations* will be a source of comfort and inspiration, both for our generation, and for generations to come in the new millennium.

Poetry is a coat of many colours. Today's poets write in a limitless array of styles: traditional rhyming poetry is a s alive and kicking today as modern free-verse. Language ranges from easily accessible to intricate and elusive.

Poems have a lot to offer in our fast-paced 'instant' world. Reading poems gives us an opportunity to sit back and explore ourselves and the world around us.

Contents

Renewal	Doreen Gooch	1
Spring - For Some People	Ken Waite	2
I Am!	Marcia Elizabeth Jenkin	3
The Signpost	Sheila Margaret Parker	4
God's Creatures	F Jensen	5
What A Beautiful Sunday	Colin Taylor	6
Sweet Elysium	Windsor Hopkins	7
The Natural World	Phyllis O'Connell	8
Natureland	Betty Worley	9
Springtime	Lachlan Taylor	11
Brave New World	N Bissett	12
Life	Robert D Shooter	13
Relative Stillness	Eric Ashwell	14
God's Healing Through Spring	Sheryl Williamson	16
My Peaceful Memories	I Low	17
Spring	A O Jones	18
Spring	Florence Dean	19
A Time To Sow	David Tallach	20
Sun Of God	Ray Butt	21
Euphony Of Summer	Janet Tinkler	22
The Sound Of Nature	Paul Duddles	23
Winter	Diane Campbell	24
Nature Is Such A Wonderful Thing	Christopher Higgins	25
Butterfly	Pat Marsh	26
Creation	Lawrence Grey	28
God's Creation	Johann K S Brangham-Tucker	29
Why Christmas?	Jean Howell	30
Simple Things That Mean A Lot	Roland Seager	31
Take Heed	Jean Rendell	32
A Morning In Spring	Gordon Jack Crisp	33
Springtime Splendour	James Leonard Clough	34
A Summer's Day	Eunice C Squire	36
Summer	Diana Momber	37

Springtime	D L Adam	38
The Wonder Of Spring	M J Bailey	39
A Wonderful World	M B Toft	40
Part Of Creation	Jane Wood	41
Creation	Valerie Mckinley	42
Penelope Corncrake	Elizabeth Anne Scott	43
Gentle Gestures	Floriana F Hall	45
New Life	M J Cudmore	46
The Special Child	Patricia Lawson	47
Around The World	Sylvia Bryan	48
The Problem	R D Hiscoke	49
The Blackbird's Song	Barbara Robson	50
Yes, The Lord God Made Them All	R A Wenn	51
Who Has The Key To Heaven?	Stella Askew	53
Just One World	Keith L Powell	54
Let There Be Light - Genesis 1.4 -	Austin Cooper	55
May Day	Joan Plant	57
The Wind	Lara Ewuosho	58
She Embraced God's Gift With Her Tender Heart	Peter James O'Rourke	59
Gazehounds	Francis Arthur Rawlinson	60
St Mungo	Janine Fitzpatrick	61
Spring Time	V B D'Wit	62
Seasons - Winter	Grace Wade	63
Springtime	Trevor Rampley	64
Waiting	Jack Lowe	65
For Ever And Ever	Joyce Atkinson	67
Untitled	Jae Willis	68
By A Creator	John Amsden	69
A Christ Offering	Patrick Davies	70
Britspring	David A Chamberlain	72
Creation	Susan Mary Robertson	73
Creation	Kathleen Poulton	74
Untitled	Pauline Haggett	75
Creation	Mary Frances Mooney	76
All Creation	Steve Newbury	77

Did God?	David Shields	78
Creation	Barry Broadmeadow	79
Garden Secret	Elizabeth Gwilliam	80
My Little Primrose	Yvone Tyerman	81
Heaven On Earth	E D Sulston	83
In The Beginning	S Groom	84
Today's World	Dorothy Ronald	86
Nature's Song	Joan Heybourn	87
Creations	Barbara Goode	89
God's Creation: An Expression Of Love	John Williams	90
Icy Fingers	J Millington	91
The Oak Tree	Linda Brown	92
The Chestnut Tree	Hilda Jones	94
Thoughts In A Garden	Fred Norgrove	95
The Announcement Of Spring	Irene Grahame	96
Lovely Day	Brenda Norman	97
The Miracle	Lilian Hellam	98
Gifts Galore	Dorothy Whitehall	99
Gentle Stranger	A J Marshall	100
Tiny Miracles	Mary Beth Bott	101
Creation	Betty M Varley	103
God's Small Miracles	Pauline Chambers	104
Leaves	Margaret Pearce	105
Creation Speaks	Brenda Ford	106
Joys Of Spring	Alma Montgomery Frank	107
Spring Banners	Pauline Pullan	109
The Crucial Six Days - Mirablile Dictu!	Welch Jeyaraj Balasingam	110
We Are All In The Making, We Are All God's Creation	Siobhan O'Conchubhair	111
God's Creation	Kathleen Glover	112
Restart	J Williams	113
The Restless Sea	Eileen Chamberlain	114
My Wonderful Land	Barry Cregg	115
The Thread	Ann Ebbs	116
Gifts Of Grace	Mary Brechemier	117
Snow	B R Winbolt	118

Springtime	Sheila A Waterhouse	119
A Precious Gift	Dorothy White	120
Our Planet Home The Silent War	Peter Manson-Herrod	121
Life	Colin Winfield	123
Untitled	J Miller	125
By The Thames At Sunset	Harriette Lewis	126
To Creation	Christine Hare	127
Season's Symphonies	Elsie Francis	128
Two's Company Three's A Family	Jenny Elton	129
Eden	Chris Moat	130
Just A Thought	Daisy Helen Thompson	131
Isabella Plantation: God's Glory Glimpsed	Nina Helene	132
The Four Seasons	Neil McClafferty	134
First Impression	Norma Christina Robson	135
Taraxacum Officinale	Oonagh Twomey	136
The Perfect Wait	W Stanbury	137
Singing	Robert D Hayward	138
Sunset	Barbara Anne Smith	140
The Ela#1tion Of Creati#2on	David John Dunbar	141
The Snows Of Spring	Frances Gibson	142
The Creator	Dorothy Ventris	143
All Seasons Have A Message	Doreen Barwell	145
The Gift	K White	146
Cat	Catherine Gregory	147
Freedom	Pauline Dodworth	148
Creation	Mandy Harvey	149
Summer	A R Frape	151
Seasonal Changes	Kevin McCann	152
Surrounded By His Love	Linda Roberts	153
God's Creation	H M Regan	154
God's World	Brenda Russell	155
Beautiful Garden	Dawn Harwood	156
Snow Drops A Legend	Rosalind Taylor	157
When God Created Woman	Patricia M Kenyon	159
The Wedding	Cordelia D Adams	160

Reason For Living	R Martin	162
God	P OFE	163
Our Miracle	Lilian Roundhill	164
Before The Time Of Greed	R Bishop	165
Words Of Jesus	Irene Spencer	166
Memories	Jessica Davies	167
The Eve Of Creation	Jeanette Latta	168
Precious Moments	Vera M Coote	169
The Wonder Of You	Robert Beach	170
Creation	Jean de Leon Mason	171
February Refugees	Manfred Reuser	172
The Bluebell Wood	Wendy Allen	173
A Moment Of Magic	Connie Huntingdon	174
Swallow	Inga Hass	175
Reflecting On A Drive Through The Trough Of Bowland	Elizabeth Leslie	176
Awakenings	Colin Zarhett	177
Tinitis Blues	Elwyn Johnson	178
Birth Of Janice	William D H Cook	179

Renewal

Spring is my most favourite time of year
With all things new starting to appear
Nature cleverly leaves old things behind
As it creates new life to please even the saddest mind
It's also the humbling time of lent
When the Son of God into the wilderness spent
Time reflecting, and rejecting temptation
Usefully using the time in meditation
In my own life I've spent many years
Wandering in the wilderness with all my fears
Regretting, worrying and struggling to find
An escape, a solution, some peace of mind
To get my life back on track
And forget the bad things that kept knocking me back
I've turned back to my faith and the years I'd lost
Coming out of the wilderness, realising the cost
Of the years I'd wandered aimlessly about
Living in fear, worry and doubt
All that's now past as of today
Spring has arrived for me, and come May
I'll trust God more fully, and learn to love Him better
My days in the wilderness are now gone forever.

Doreen Gooch

Spring - For Some People

They say the yellow daffodils
Are now above the ground,
And that the red camelias
Are starting to abound.

I hear the mating calls of birds
That fly from tree to tree.
I'm told their joyous cavortings
Are quite a sight to see.

I feel the warmth of longer days
And know that winter's gone,
And that this world's a lovely place
To gaze and dwell upon.

I read of 'maids sprig-muslin drest'
In Hardy set in Braille,
And Browning's 'Home Thoughts' conjure up
Fresh beauties to regale

My sightless and frustrated eyes,
But what folk really see
To waken them with glad surprise
Are mysteries to me.

The artistries that God designed
Enhance, if anything,
The agony of being blind
When it is Spring.

Ken Waite

I Am!

I am Creator of the flowers that spread
unseen perfumes!
I authorise within each head the bird's dawn
chorus tunes!
I am the organising force behind natures routine
My wise techniques used my bird's beaks, are
known & yet *unseen!*
The tiniest worm knows *when* to squirm, to
the earth's surface rising,
To take a drink when raindrops fall, does
man find this surprising?
All beasts possess maternal love, for each
must rear its young.
Protective instinct from *above* preserve
this world I run.

I am the maker of mankind, I made man's
body whole,
Gave him an independent mind, a spirit
and a soul!
Fruits of man's spirit, Joy, Love, Peace,
by words & thoughts unseen,
I transmit with my heavenly power to
souls from sin made clean

I am the author of the word, the origin
of time!

The *science* behind this universe, exclusively
is *mine!*
The elements of healing power that only
I impart,
On those believing, I endow, to each
repentant heart!

Marcia Elizabeth Jenkin

The Signpost

What does spring-time mean to you?
Birds singing, skies of blue
Colour bursting from the earth
God's promise of re-birth

Isn't His message visibly clear?
A gentle reminder each coming year
That after a lifetime of joy and strife
In death we are re-born, given a new life

As the autumn leaf decays
God is showing us the method of His ways
For after the harshness of cold winter night
Again comes the warmth, sunshine's shining light

So please stop your fighting,
Quick fixes, jealousy and hate
Expecting life be all cherries on a plate
Quietly, reverently, live your life through
Bravely facing each task He has set for you
Just like the flowers so wind tossed and blown
Stand firm to survive and follow His sign

Then, when the time comes bid the world goodbye
Your spirit will be gathered by God on high
How good to show Him you have brightened the world
Just like the spring flower your life's work unfurled.

Sheila Margaret Parker

God's Creatures

Collective nouns for animals, a rich anthology,
Compiled, it seems, at random and without apology.
We know that lions in the wild are always called a Pride,
But who would know that pheasants are referred to as a Nide.

Dolphins swim in Schools, we know, just the same as whales,
But rarely do we hear about a Watch of nightingales.
Among the larger animals there's a Sloth of bears,
Among the many smaller ones there's a Husk of hares.

A term not often heard is Kindle, which applies to kittens.
And yet another one is Siege, a gathering of Bitterns.
Other birds, the housemartins, gather in a Richesse,
While, of all the primates, apes cohabit in a Shrewdness.

We humans warrant various nouns, some which do us proud.
Usually we're spoken of as being just a Crowd.
But when we're dominated by the bully or the yob,
Then we're relegated to that odious term - a Mob.

F Jensen

What A Beautiful Sunday

The solid aged oak stands alone,
Majestic against the blue, blue sky
And the whiteness of the snowy earth.
A thousand Romeo's walk their Juliet's
On this morning of glory.

The wind blew fresh and strong,
So dutifully the winter blooms danced
Vibrant and carefree in their routine.
Bright coloured birds serenade young lovers
On this beautiful Sunday.

Colin Taylor

Sweet Elysium

I didn't say thank you yesterday;
And I didn't pray to-day.
And the older I get;
The more I forget,
The things in life I ought to say.

I wasn't grateful for a new day beginning;
As the day began to dawn.
I didn't notice the birds sweet chorus;
As they welcomed in the morn.

I had somehow missed the flowers;
And the river on it's way.
And how the bubbling laughter of children;
Brings a smile to whatever is grey.

I had failed to appreciate others;
Which in life is a cardinal sin.
I made light of their joys and aspirations,
And thought the world in me did begin.

I'd forgotten how sweet rain tasted;
After picnics on hot summer days.
And the smell of the earth,
In the springtime.
'I now marvel at nature and her ways'.

Like great mists from the sea,
That engulf us.
Or a sky with no limit to see;
The ways of the world are beyond us;
I say thank you for your mystery.

Windsor Hopkins

The Natural World

We never really noticed the seasons during the war
Same routine, sirens, work, friends and family
All closely united and friendly

But the memory of grabbing a walk across
Hampstead Heath, Parliament Hill or Regent's Park
On those wonderful unspoiled summer days
Leaves you in a glorious haze

I remember walking with Bill before the invasion in Ken Wood
So natural, not a sole around, and way in
The distance the siren would sound

God must have sent those beautiful days with the sun kissing
Your cheek and the breeze telling you all is not lost
Let us ignore the siren so far away
Maybe this time far away it will stay

Far away maybe it will stay
To give us a break this beautiful day

Not wishing for someone else to suffer
But to make up for the long dark nights we had to rush our
Supper

To head off to the Anderson shelter, Brewery, Underground
Which one to choose depending on how bad it got
Little 'Maples' furniture store with the bench inside the
Door
With the door always open helped a lot
To rest before we carried on, so we could look forward to
Another spring
With those longer evenings, what a wonderful thing.

Phyllis O'Connell

Natureland

I love to see all tigers in their majestic splendour.
Hippo's afloat in sun mud soaked
waters, surrounded by birds of every flock.
Lion's hunting for food for their young.
What a beautiful sight they make, when
they are on the run.
Natives with spears, and strong young
legs.
Hunting all beast, so their young
can be fed.
My favourite is the Elephant, so gentle
yet so strong.
Putting their trunks into waters,
then shooting into the air.
Spurting water on everyone.
Nature is so very wonderful.
God put all animals here on
earth.
The wonders of it all, has amazed
me I think since my birth.
Zebra's so elegant, so fashionable are the
stripes.
Pelican's, beautiful birds could be
ballerina's, so graceful are their limbs.
Monkey's make me laugh, as they scramble
up and along the trees.
Dropping the odd coconuts onto the
ground below.
Then looking around so carefully,
as if to say, don't touch that, it
belongs to me!
Rhino's are a little scary, large strong
beasts so proud.
Every bird imaginable, in colours
so divine.
God really showed us he loved us,

when he put these animals here
with us.
For us to protect and care for them.
Like 'St Francis' did too.
Oh! Nature is so very wonderful
what a sight Noah's Ark must have
been animals in every form two by two.

Betty Worley

Springtime

The spring is here you can hear the bird calls
In the early morning just as the dew falls
From their perch up in the willows
They awaken folks from off their pillows.

Spring is the season which to treasure
It gives us joys in no small measure
All the buds have started peeping
From out the earth where they've been sleeping

The snowdrops and the daffodils
Have escaped the winters icy chills
And now their colours can be seen
Blossoming amid this springtime scene.

Spring is the end of hibernation
When sleeping giants find liberation
And plant life than begins to thrive
As the ground around becomes alive.

Lachlan Taylor

Brave New World

Farewell, then, to mahogany and teak,
Magnificent in greens and golden browns,
Palawan narrawood, oak, elm and ash,
All lovely trees that ever were since time began,
Logged to extinction, lashed by toxic rain,
With poisoned roots and charnel crowns,
Murdered by axe and chainsaw, slash
And burn, the field of battle desolate and bleak.

To ibex, panther, panda, leopard, lion,
Farewell, farewell to tiger and orang-utan,
Tusked pachyderms of grave, primeval majesty,
United with diplodocus and mastodon,
Sating the axe's lust. Mountains of bone,
For ornaments or Chinese potency,
Obscure the blood-red plains that turn
The hunters' hands and hearts incarnidine.

To porpoise, tuna, whale and albacore,
Farewell, farewell to shoals that darted, dived and played
In swarming multitudes. They used to teem
Around these shores - mackerel, herring, cod,
Salmon that were the handiwork of God,
His bounty. Nets snared the living stream,
Exhausting it, and now the creels, decayed,
Shall gather in rich harvests never more.

Farewell to all the songbirds of the sky,
Which once performed the symphony of the wealds:
Nightingale, blackbird, skylark, linnet, thrush,
Wagtail and willow warbler, robin, wren.
No hedgerow forms their headstone, and no bush.
The ploughs and pesticides of greedy men
Have scattered silent death across the fields
And sepulchred in rape their corpses lie.

N Bissett

Life

God blew
form into void
giving life to all through
His Kingdom in the universe;
share fair.

Robert D Shooter

Relative Stillness

On a restful morning there is peace and stillness,
in the sunny garden in late spring;
The flowers are varied and in freshness,
With youth and eternity in the air pervading.

The early bee garners the nectared treasure,
The natural order of foliage is disciplined and sure;
Seemingly things go on as they were before,
And to the mind nothing alters to upset the heavenly pleasure.

Yet everything is in motion,
The petal of the proud but modest bloom
Is a whirl of atomic revolution;
The roots themselves circling in the planetary gyration.

The sun is the only fixed object about,
But even its warmth and pleasant radiation
Moves at the high speed of light;
Which with earthly reposition fades at night.

There is passage of time also in the yearly round,
The cycle of growth and decay with rebirth;
Another example of change to be found
In the soil out of sight and sound.

On our spinning wheel of life we stay our set years;
But are later cast off with many sad tears,
By the worldly centrifuge which requires
Youth and a tight grip to realise our desires.

Let us hope there is always perpetual motion,
The intermeshing of many a varied revolution;
More than enough to overcome misspent misdirection,
Slowing down all things by contrary action.

Eric Ashwell

God's Healing Through Spring

This poem shows God's love and care
Here many happy syllables are recorded,
Telling how spring is now everywhere,
And God's gifts through spring, are given; not hoarded,
Drawing pictures in your mind,
That God carefully designed.

Now birds sing, and flowers abound
God shows his detailed expression,
By showing newness all around,
New life appears, its own perfection,
God's creative work revealed,
Everywhere is healed.

God shows through spring, how he remakes,
By shaping with divine expression.
Winter's barren land then forsakes,
Its crumbling shell, to a lively procession
Of re-birth. God revealed.
His spring has healed!

Sheryl Williamson

My Peaceful Memories

My favourite place is Letham Glen
When as a little girl I can recall is when
There were go-as-you-please competitions
Many happy times spent on the putting green

You could go to pet's corner
Now this just had to be seen
There were all kinds of birds, monkeys
and rabbits too.
It was a wonderful place, plenty to do.
Walk through the gardens, gorgeous
flowers galore.
Over the bridges to see what more
was in store
Rhododendron bushes, lovely roses
as well
Flowers of fantastic colours with a
wonderful smell
Sit on the bench seat and have a
wee think
Sun streamed through the trees and
sometimes it'd blink
Or maybe just talk and reminisce
With all this beauty - ah! - wasn't
it bliss
It's no wonder I like the Glen
Its joys never cease
My own special place
With its own inner peace.

I Low

Spring

Once more it is spring,
that glorious season;
a heavenly thing
that's sent with good reason.
It shows us the goodness and glory of God.

It freshens the land
and inspires mankind.
How well does His hand
refresh ev'ryone's mind
with the newness and the beauty of all things in spring!

A O Jones

Spring

The trees are stark and bare against the sky,
The air is chill, the snowflakes gently fall.
The garden looks so desolate and forlorn,
Can it be now that the seeds of spring are born?

The snowdrops hang their heads in innocence.
Fresh and tender spears break through the ground.
The snow is melting and the river's high.
Can it be that spring is almost nigh?

Birdsong, insistent and triumphant, greets the dawn,
Trees wear a gauzy film of gay, green lace.
The hedgerows burst with vibrant cheer.
The spring, the long-awaited spring is here.

Florence Dean

A Time To Sow

The light is coming, flexing its fingers,
Preparing to throw aside the dark coverlet of winter.
Hidden bulbs in the sleeping earth flower
In underground resistance to the autocratic cold.
Already their petals are blooming in defiance,
Sending forth their liberation armies of colour.

The fledgling brightness gains in strength,
Learning to stretch its wings against the dark.
The seeding season blossoms all around,
Tractors rumbling as they scatter gifts
To be returned many times over come harvest.
Bright-eyed birds line their nests and wait.

David Tallach

Sun Of God

The sun is only over the hill; it is here, as it was yesterday and will be tomorrow, but never somewhere else.

In a bespoken global overcoat
It hides behind a weighty cloud,
Stretching far beyond our vision
A sepulchral, all embracing shroud.

Or across some vague horizon
It takes an early morning roll,
Arriving high in time for lunch
And a distant evening stroll.

Then, shimmering yellow haze is gone,
Last remnants of the audience dispersed
And light is dimmed to glowing red
With grey and violet hush and all immersed.

Solar mission now accomplished here
It moves to bake some other earthy crust
And yet, reliable as a life-long friend
It leaves a lunar luminosity in trust.

Another day, but not another sun,
The self-same yellow ball of fire returns
Donating permeating fleshy warmth
To banish all our deep concerns.

Ray Butt

Euphony Of Summer

Clear crystal stream, tenderly flowing,
Soothingly rippling o'er pebbles worn smooth,
Above, vibrant skylark spiralling upwards,
Filling the air with his boisterous song.

On soft warm earth, field mice gleefully playing,
Scurrying, rustling, midst waving ears of corn,
Lambs bleating joyously in lush green pastures,
Gambolling fleet of foot, energy unbound.

Excited drone of Honey-bee, from flower to flower,
Collecting sweet nectar, flitting home to hive,
Chirruping crickets 'neath fragrant lively hedgerows,
In clement motion leaves whisper softly in trees.

Harmonious feeling of spiritual tranquillity,
As long golden days drift serenely along,
A time for reflection in peaceful meditation,
Accompanied by the honeyed, euphony of summer.

Janet Tinkler

The Sound Of Nature

Listen to the wind
Blowing through the trees
Creaking branches and dropping twigs
And the rustling of the leaves
Listen to the rain
Dropping from the sky
Falling on the roof tops
From so way up high
Listen to the snow
Settling on the ground
Listen very, very hard
It hardly makes a sound
Listen to the sun
Drying the morning dew
Listen for the hissing
Of the pavement drying too
Listen to the birdsong
As night gives way to dawn
Hear the world come to life
As we reach another morn
Listen to the waves
As they crash onto the beach
Listen to the children laughing
As it wets their tiny feet
Listen to the country sounds
The insects, wasps and bees
Listen to the gentle whisper
Of a summer breeze
Listen to the sounds of nature
Hear the sounds of life
Listen to the sounds of people
It's good to be alive

Paul Duddles

Winter

The Winter is long and cold.
The sun shine's a watery gold,
How I wish the Summer was here,
To feel the heat from the sun,
The Winter is long and cold,
The frost's are harsh and cruel,
No sign's of Spring, with bud's opening,
No fresh green leaves on the tree's.
Just the snow, gently falling around,
The Winter is long and cold,
The wind chill's you to the bone,
Dare you go out in the wind,
Dare you go out alone,
I long for Spring and Summer,
Long hot, sun-shiny day's,
Lazing about in the meadow,
Basking in the heat haze,
The Winter is long and cold, I'm feeling old,
I wait for Summer sunshine, of Bright gold.

Diane Campbell

Nature Is Such A Wonderful Thing

The way that nature is such a wonderful thing,
the way that the flowers bloom, and the birds sing,
the way the warm sun, and the cool winds caress,
the way the creatures of the world draw breath,
the way the plants and trees just grow and grow,
the way that the rivers and lakes ebb and flow,
the way that snow and rain will fall with grace,
the way that the planet Earth turns endlessly in space,
the way that mountains and hills stand proud, so high,
the way they compliment the clouds within the sky,
the way the seas and oceans are so very deep,
the way the starry sky passes you by, as you sleep,
the way each fresh morning, a brand new day is born,
the way the bright sunlight welcomes another dawn.

Christopher Higgins

Butterfly

The dance of the butterfly
Sings of joy,
Sings of beauty
And of peace,
Mirrors the wonder
Of the transformation in our lives.

Within a dark chrysalis
A life lies dormant;
In a dark chrysalis which is so small,
So insignificant,
So tiny in the hands of the Creator,
As it hangs unnoticed and uncared for.

Yet,
Deep within, a caterpillar is dying,
Dying to self;
Changing
In the warmth of God's embrace.

Slowly, patiently, secretly
Being transformed
Until
In His own way and His own time
A new life
Is ready to be revealed.

And when the timing is Just Right
For the great Creator's plan,
The new life breaks free.
Beauty is revealed,
Created from the ordinariness of a dusty chrysalis.

Nervously at first,
Uncertain of the fragility of the newness which it feels,
Slowly, trustingly,
The wings of the butterfly
Open themselves fully
To the sunshine of God's love.
And as the healing rays of love
Strengthen those fragile wings
New confidence is born.
The butterfly takes off
In a dance of joyous celebration,
Radiantly reflecting back to the world
The beauty
And the love
Of God.

Pat Marsh

Creation

Was it God that caused the big bang?
Into the universe to spray,
Expanding gas and elements.
But who created DNA?

Lawrence Grey

God's Creation

I stood on the hill above the rolling plain
And saw the mist rising after the morning rain;
The rays of the sun warmed the sodden ground,
Making the mist rise upward bound.
The air was sweet, fresh, and clean,
And across the valley could be seen, a rainbow!
With its colours bright, stretching away out of sight;
And down in the valley could also be seen
A silver river like a narrow stream,
Winding its way through field and fenn,
Then doubling back on itself again.

Waking flowers by the sun-rays kissed,
Tips of trees peeping through the mist;
Skylarks singing high in the sky,
Busy bees, wandering butterflies;
Cattle grazing in lush fields of green,
And over yonder could be seen,
Young lambs, bounding in twos and threes
Disturbing the butterflies and the bees;
And it made me think of the power that must be,
To have created this beauty, that surrounded me.

Johann K S Brangham-Tucker

Why Christmas?

'What is the reason for Christmas,
Please tell me Mother dear.
Why do we remember Christmas
At each and every year?'
'My darling child, I'm sure you know,
The reason it is clear,
For Jesus Christ was born that day
A baby oh so dear'.
'So why was his birth important,
Please tell me Mother dear
And why do we still celebrate
Each and every year?'
'A sweet and tiny baby boy
Was born upon that day
To teach us all that God is love
And to live in Our Lords way.
So live your life as you were taught,
With love, compassion too,
Keeps Gods commandments in your heart
As He gave his Son to do.
For Goodness, Love and Mercy,
Will stand you in good stead
Never, ever, forget that Baby,
Asleep in his stable bed.
For he came to be our beacon
To guide us all our days,
The greatest gift mankind could have
To help us in life's ways'.

Jean Howell

Simple Things That Mean A lot

For the fascinating fire fly
And the majestic craggy rocks
To the small and rippling brooks
And the wide mysterious lochs
The shy and scented violets
Set in their mossy banks
To these as part of God's work
I give my humble thanks

The brilliance of the rainbow
A beauty to behold
Daffodils in the wind
A patch of dancing gold
The rich song of the singing bird
Contentment of the lowing herd
The colour of the butterfly
Communion 'tween God and I

The rich brown earth
That's newly tilled
The poppies in the summer field
The joy to see, the rolling hills
White clouds, dark clouds all the thrills
To see the gentle falling rain
Make tears upon the window pane
The trees, the treasures of the earth
To all of this, our God gave birth

Roland Seager

Take Heed

When we are no longer here
The daffodils will still appear
So let's enjoy every moment
And hold life's miracles of nature dear
The Narcissi, Crocus and Tulip
Serve only to remind us
That life's problems are really only a blip
So in our hurry make sure we do not miss life's bus
Blackbird, Robin and Thrush
Spare not a moment in their rush
To fulfil life's plan for them
They do not spend a day in wasted thought
But rather wisely try to avoid being caught
So let us learn natures lesson
Enjoy what we have today
Otherwise we could all end up losing our way
Be like those garden birds
Have our life's plan in mind
Be happy peaceful and kind
Or we could be laid to rest, only remembered in words.

Jean Rendell

A Morning In Spring

When it's warm on a morning in spring
I sit in the garden upon the swing
There's an infants school some way away
I can hear the children come out to play
The distant sound of a garden mower
Sometimes hand-pushed, sometimes power
The sound of the trains way over the hill
They go through the cutting, then all is still
The warmth of the sun, the sound of the bees
I feel the newspaper fall off my knees
Oh yes! I do doze for a minute or two
It's something I confess I find easy to do
To awake and thrill to the song of a wren
Is to marvel at nature - free to all men
And just to listen to the song of a bird
Is surely the sweetest sound to be heard
The 'pink' of a blackbird on seeing a cat
Warning his mate on her nest in a hat
There's four groups of crows that call to each other
Quavering call from youngster, firm 'caw' from mother
'Peeps' from the blue tits twelve in a brood
The 'chack' of the magpie, so vicious and rude
I hear the yaffle, that's his country name
Laughs like a kookaburra, but not so insane
The 'mew' of the pigeon flying back to the nest
The monotonous 'coo' of its mate is a sound I detest
A flock of sparrows fly down all a-squabble
Bathing starling flies off, wings all a-wobble
And all the other birds I can hear but not see
Yes, the sounds of the birds means so much to me.

Gordon Jack Crisp

Springtime Splendour

The beauty of earth,
Ethereal skies;
The wonder of birth,
Gladden eager eyes.
The everlasting sea,
Living green spring days,
Creation's bounty free;
Life giver we praise.

The cloud's gentle rain,
Healthful winds, warm sun;
Nourish growing grain,
Blessing everyone.
The cattle on the land,
Singing birds on wing;
Toddlers playing with sand,
Welcome fairest spring.

Springtime wakes grey gloom,
In woodland and field;
Opens snowdrops' bloom,
Bluebells in the Weald.
Purple heather on moors,
With dawn fresh and bright;
The sweet primrose lures,
Hours of pure delight.

On rolling meadows,
Frisky lambs now play.
Sun chases shadows,
Swiftly o'er pathway.
Burgeon downy violets,
Near the winding stream;
Lapwings plunge on islets,
For insects where they teem.

Blend with pure Nature,
Hear each rustling tree;
Rest in its rapture,
Rejoice in high glee.
No more noisy clatter,
Smiling spring has won.
Such charms never batter,
Blossom-time what fun!

James Leonard Clough

A Summer's Day

See the poppies growing
By the wayside fair,
Celandine and buttercup
Too, are growing there.
Daisies, thistles, ragwort,
Are also blooming too.
Birds up in the treetops
Sing for me and you.

Mountains in the distance
Stand erect and still,
The river flows so softly
By the old windmill.
Clouds above are rolling
Wind blowing up for rain,
All this beauty needs it,
Just to refresh again.

Then thunderclouds start banging,
Fiery lights across the sky,
The trees sap up the water
Then hang their leaves to dry.
After storm and rainclouds
The sun comes out once more,
All dries up so quickly,
Then we're happy as before.

For we can go awalking
Among the fields so green,
We hear the crickets chirping,
The grass has a brighter sheen.
The cows are in the meadow,
The sheep are on the hill,
We can rest in quietness,
For all is calm and still

Eunice C Squire

Summer

Sunshine and silence everywhere. High noon
Blazes across the shimmering fields of flowers;
The hazy, golden heat of cloudless June.
From the tall grasses pollen drifts in showers.

The quiet is made of little murmuring sounds;
Whirring of hidden wings; the hum of bees;
And a low thunder through the hush resounds,
The far off rise and fall of slumbering seas.

Peace on the hills; calm on the distant plain.
Forgotten, loss and weariness and strife;
That autumn storms must come with cold, grey rain;
That shadows fall across all earthly life.

Sun and deep silence. This is surely given,
These days - green islands in rainbowed sea -
This wide blue sky, to be a glimpse of heaven;
This beauty, part of the great mystery.

So is the ageless song of the earth heard
Through silent sunshine. Amid grasses thin
The soft wind dies; from woods no singing bird:
Only the tide of summer surges in.

Diana Momber

Springtime

The trees are full of blossom
The hedge fresh shades of green
Where'er you cast your eyes about
There's beauty to be seen.

The suns not always shining
The soil needs lots of rain
Co's if it's always sunshine
The flowers won't bloom again.

Count snow and rain as blessings
As they fall upon the land
Enjoy each coming season
That makes this earth so grand.

D L Adam

The Wonder Of Spring

As I awake and look at the beauty of the land,
Created by God by his own hand,
As the sun shines bright'ly in the sky above,
The birds singing songs of love.

The flowers starting to sprout and grow,
From the seeds that have been sown,
Daffodils and roses also bloom,
There colours removing all thoughts of gloom,
There scent pleasant in the air,
Making live easier and life to bare,
For all around the world to share.

The trees with there blossoms,
Are a sight to behold,
The beauty of God a wonder to be told,
There is so much for the eyes to focus,
Violets, primroses, bluebells, and crocus.

But the true wonder is the gift of life,
A new baby born to both Man and Wife,
The bleating of new born lambs,
Jumping around the fields so green,
No lovelier sight to be seen.

Thank you Father for your gifts so true,
The sky above so bright and blue,
All from God who loves us so true.

M J Bailey

A Wonderful World

It's a wonderful world you created
The green rolling fields and the flowers
The trees in their glory
They all tell your story
You made all these things ! And there ours

It's a wonderful world you created
The birds as they sing in the trees
The fish in the sea
As they swim wild and free
The warmth of the soft summer breeze

It's a wonderful world you created
The sun rising up! Not a sound
The full moon at night
The stars shining bright
There's beauty and peace all around

It's a wonderful world you created
The rain belting down from above
The cold and the snow
When it's twenty below
We'll be filled with your warmth and your love

It's a wonderful world you created
A pussy cat! Dog! Kangaroo
A big fuzzy bear, he hasn't a care
We've got all these things! Thanks to you

It's a wonderful world you created
The houses, the church with its steeple
It seems such a shame
But that's why you came
The world got messed up! By the people

M B Toft

Part Of Creation

The Earth is mine, all mine,
For I am part of it.
I am not a being, separate, and all alone.
The air I breathe becomes a part of me.
I drink the water of Life.
My eyes see all the beauty of the Earth.
It is imprinted on my mind.
The sounds heard by my ears
Become the music of my soul.
And things I touch become a part
Of the fibre of my being.
What joy it is to be at peace,
And to be at one with the Earth,
And so, also with the Eternal Universe.

Jane Wood

Creation

Fill each minute as you would fill each day
full to the brim with life.
Let not one single second waste away,
do not cheapen it with strife.
As each and every precious moment goes,
make it count for all it's worth.
Appreciate what Mother Nature knows
God's masterpiece . . . is Earth.

Valerie Mckinley

Penelope Corncrake

Struttling and strattling, scuffing and scratching,
Kicking up dust while parading and catching
The eye of every cock in the yard.
Showing off plumage and trying so hard
To appear so grand and to be avant-garde.
Nothing has felt so good and so rare.
'I am the best' I do declare.
See the breeze flutter in my coat,
Rippling the colours as I stretch my throat,
I let forth a call to tell all about
'I'm here and I'm waiting'. Without a doubt.
The world has erupted, I'm ready for love.
Spring is here and the blue skies above
Summon the happiness of the country around.
The farm, the meadow, the fields and the sound
Of the new lambs bleating and the wild birds singing.

They call me Penolope, the folks in the house,
Look after us well by all accounts.
She feeds me by hand and strokes me so good,
And tells me she's looking towards a brood
Of lovely fine chicks in a few days time,
But to please her this way- the pleasure's all mine.
I have my eye on the cockerel there,
The one with the comb and the arrogant air,
The one who crows at the crack of dawn,
And fills me with passion as we share the corn.
We peck 'round the farmyard and flirt and flight,
To see us dancing 'tis a wonderful sight.
I'll lead him astray, in my own clever way,
And as usual I'll have him without delay.
But must dash off now for the eggs are cooling,
Leave him looking, and panting and drooling.
I'll hatch out my family and then I'll be free
To give him my life and then we'll see
What is this enigma what we have heard

Is passing around from word to word
That we farm animals are not prepared
For things to come, and some feared,
Especially us chickens in our prime
What is this thing called 'Coq au Vin?'

Elizabeth Anne Scott

Gentle Gestures

Comforting is the gentle rain,
Pitter-patter on the window pane,
Nourishing nature's gifts of sustenance,
Gardens, plants and trees in abundance.

Considerate is the gentle man,
Tender, kind, who takes your hand
And lifts you up, body and soul
When circumstances exist beyond control.

Sensitive is the gentle woman,
Understanding, attentive, softly spoken,
Soothing furrowed brows of mankind,
Manners, morals, respect and love defined.

Sweetness is the gentle child,
Caring, sharing all the while
Obeying the ten commandments of God
From morning to night's refreshing nod.

Placid is the gentle wind,
Unruffled, calm and disciplined,
Seeds of germination midst the storms -
God's gifts come in many forms.

Floriana F Hall

New Life

What can I say about the new life that we have,
In all shapes and forms, new life is giving to us.
When God created the earth oh? What beauty he gave,
From the heavens to the earth, to give us new birth.

The birds that fly, High, and the fish that swim,
All the animals that move, God gave to them new life.
Then he made man from dust, he breathed in him new life.
Then because man was lonely, he made a woman for him to
share

In the Garden of Eden, God put Adam and Eve.
To flourish and to grow, together in there new life.
We can have new life, if we learn to love,
The God who made us, and gave us love anew.

When we let Jesus into our lives, we then can be reborn,
To wash away the old, and then bring in the new.
When this is done and we are set free from sin,
Then we can turn around and say, Thank You Lord for the New
Life that you gave to me. Amen

M J Cudmore

The Special Child

A lovely new baby, content as could be.
Her mother, she sobbed and cried, 'God, why me?'
Lying there in her cot - life of simplicity,
This little child born with a disability.

God answered back, 'Pull yourself together,
To this precious small child, you are very clever.
It is you I have chosen to give so much love,
Be kind and be patient with my little dove.'

The mother she cried till she could cry no more,
Help her she must - she would learn to adore.
This little wee mite - her own flesh and blood,
As the years flew past, she became very glad.

Together they had learned to love one another,
Progress quite slow, but with praise from her mother.
This precious child in her own little world
brought happiness and joy - A Special Child!

Patricia Lawson

Around The World

I have a little sailing boat
Just like a proper one
And I sail it in the rock pools
And I have alot of fun

For when the sun is shining
I go down to the sands
Then I pretend I'm sailing
Far away to foreign lands

I'm sailing all around the world
In sunshine and in rain
But when it comes to supper time
I've landed home again.

I went out on the shore again
My Mummy said I could
If I'd be very careful
So I promised her I would

I took my little boat with me
It only is a toy
Then I put it in the water
And I called out Ship A Hoy

It sailed away so gaily
That I thought I was afloat
Fishing in the deep sea waters
In my little sailing boat.
But soon the sun was sinking
And I had to make my way
Back home to tea and thinking
I'd come out another day

Sylvia Bryan

The Problem

It's such a great big puzzle to me and I don't know what to do
And I'm trying all I can to put it right
For I love my darling pussy and I love the birdies too
And yesterday I had a dreadful fright
The birds were busy pecking the crumbs I'd thrown outside
It really is surprising what a lot they want to eat
And I'm sure they chirped their 'thank you' as they hopped from side
to side
And seemed to think the dry bread quiet a treat
I sat and watch them eating and pussy watched them too
When suddenly she gave a fearful spring
And quicker even than I spy to teacher 'twice one's two'
They flew away and chirped like anything
Now I love my darling pussy I love her more and more
And I want her to have every thing that's nice
And I am sure she must be tired of cats meat in tins
Just the same I'm tired of eating plain boiled rice
So it's all a great big puzzle an' I've thought it out all day
For I like my darling pussie to have some thing good to eat
And yet I clapped my hands to see those birdies fly away
Instead of being gobbled up like meat

R D Hiscoke

The Blackbird's Song

He sang before the break of morn
Daisy eyes still shut upon the lawn.
Such range, spontaneity of song
In warm sun I'm swept along
No diva has such range of note
As from the blackbirds tiny throat
Bending low I smell spring earth
All life around has given birth
Sing happy bird now I perceive
My own heart is filled with joie de vivre

Barbara Robson

Yes, The Lord God Made Them All

Propped up in bed I listen, as night is breaking dawn,
and from my bedroom window, I see a springtime morn,
like me, the sun is rising, adding crimson to each cloud,
what I hear is wonderful; the 'dawn chorus' oh so loud.

Birds are taking to the wing, 'tis the start of another day,
they go off in search of food, worms slugs and other prey,
just watching God's creations, this includes birds of the air,
is worth that daily struggle, from the bed to my wheelchair.

Sitting out in the morning sun, the air is fresh and clean,
across the fens I see arable land, and pastures oh so green,
frolicking in the meadow, two spring lambs newly born,
gentle as the morning dew, fresh as the first kiss of dawn.

'Korrk kok' the cock pheasant calls, from yonder field of wheat,
he's courting three young hen birds, who think he's rather sweet,
overhead a magpie; 'Chack chack' not letting the pheasants rest,
he is on reconnaissance, preparing to steal eggs from their nest.

My water garden attracts many birds, a place to bathe and feed,
a varied choice on a menu, of bread, nuts, and mixed seed,
some birds are very trusting, they will call you now and then,
I listen to the 'Tic tic tic', that's my little friend the jenny wren.

Foraging beneath the primula, looking for insects to eat,
is the petite little dunnock, constantly calling 'Tseep tseep',
this wakens the slumbering bull frog, who lets out a mighty croak,
then takes refuge on a lily pad, with looks that say 'This is no joke'.

The heat of the day's upon us, to the fenman it's 'High Noon',
and rest assured the wagtails, will be dropping in quite soon,
the yellow and pied wagtails, gnats and flies their favourite dish,
that's why they hover by the fountain, in the pond that has the fish.

The collar doves have just arrived 'Coo coo cook' they call,
serving notice they've come to bathe, in the cool of the waterfall
the sparrows and the starlings, always seem to be in a rush,
unlike the elegant blackbird, and the beautiful old song thrush.

The world is full of beautiful things, for one and all to hear or see,
my life is spent in a wheelchair, but nature means so much to me,
as do the words 'Bright and beautiful, creatures great and small',
I was taught, and will never forget; The Lord God made them all

Wenn-The-Penn

R A Wenn

Who Has The Key To Heaven?

Who has the key to Heaven
Who will let me in?
Love is the key to Heaven,
Love will open the door.

The love of God is everywhere
But we have to earn it that's clear.
For the love of God is everlasting
For those who hold Him dear.

Yes, Love is the key to Heaven
Love should rule the world.
Peace and goodwill will follow
When love has opened the door.

Stella Askew

Just One World

Just one world for us to live in
And it is spring time again
It all ways seems so new
Where nothing seems the same.

Just one world for us to live in
With new creations all around
With every thing nice to look at
And the birds making such sweet sounds.

Just one world for us to live in
And the world is a wonder of that I am sure
As well as a thing of beauty
Even an apple core.

Keith L Powell

Let There Be Light
-Genesis 1.4-

Spring . . . huge dam-burst
Of light.
Light prism-cast in pure tints,
Of crystal colour . . . light
Washed in so many greens
That no painter could imitate . . .
Purity of sound
In the first wistful grace-notes
Of a thrush high against the sky
Before his fluting sweetness of full song . . .
Ecstasy of new life in furious love making
Croaking and chirruping
Of frog and toad,
Their opalescent bubbles, dark necklaces
Spawning in the sky of the pond.

Spring . . . one all-pervading stir
Of wing in squabbling fury
Of nesting, feeding . . .
By rooks crying hoarsely from stick nests,
Hen blackbirds
Desperate under the gardener's spade
For his turned earth.

So in a night, invasion
Dam-breaking of that flood
In a sea of many yellow-greens
Throughout the flatland
And its golden river-loop of sun,
Mock sunlight in dark cart lanes
Lit by celandine,
All along the hedgerows
Hawthorn blossom
Like sea waves, breaking . . .

And who can walk sad and unbelieving
In this holy flood, blaze,
Frenzy of life starting, purpose
So hugely and widely written,
Be still untouched,
Indifferent or left with any doubt
Of a Creator's hand . . .

Austin Cooper

May Day

Weaving Patterns round a maypole,
Demure as butterflies,
Salad fresh, in their new frocks
Bought from Marks and Sparks.

Boys discover two left feet,
And do all the tripping,
Lambs and chicks come out to play,
Hawthorn rains confetti.

Somewhere a radio signals:
May Day, May Day, May Day.

Joan Plant

The Wind

We are the children of the wind
we embody its polarities
whispering in harmonies;
raging through the cyclone,
unfathomable gentleness seeps through.
Lofty fragrances ride on its wave,
a whiff of God's breath
forever we blow -
through it,
in it,
on it.
God's lullaby
bestowing power, lending peace
if its unspoken law of silence
is obeyed . . .
Sshhh - listen, can you hear its chords now?
We are the wind,
the voice of God.

Lara Ewuosho

She Embraced God's Gift With Her Tender Heart

From her crying heart came a flood of tears
Like a miracle of spring.
When she beheld for that first time
All the love a child can bring.
Pure fragile beauty in her gentle arms
God's creation and her dream,
A celebration to enfold
Like pure springtime love supreme.

How can words explain all that mother's joy
As she kissed her child that day?
When Heaven sent a blessing true
More love than sweet words portray.
She embraced God's gift with her tender heart
Precious love before her eyes,
Her soul was filled with praise and prayer
Through each sunset and sunrise.

Peter James O'Rourke

Gazehounds

I like to watch the elegance and grace
The movement and conformation of dogs that race
Summetry beholding to the eye
The sheer elegance could make you cry
Whippet and greyhound as they parade around
Like spectre ghosts without a sound
Nothing there could kinder be
To stand with its chin upon your knee
Makes you wonder in the human race
That only a dog should have such a honest face

Francis Arthur Rawlinson

St Mungo

A hand upraised
In verdigris of time,
He smiles, his sisters by his side,
And bids them read their books,
And confidently strum their joyful harps.
His hair is long in sixties-style,
And out beyond his gaze,
The fountain falls, bronze pillar, toadstool bathed in water.
Two shalwar-kamiz girls stride purposefully
To work, to learn, to earn,
This fine May morning, I'm watching all the city -
And warm between my shoulder blades, the sunrise pats my back.

Janine Fitzpatrick

Spring Time

Spring has come.
There's magic in the air,
With primroses and daffodils,
And the frolics of
The Mad March Hare.
Old winter, he's been
Laid to rest,
Gone are all
His aches and pain;
For Mother Nature
She knows best,
And has transformed
Her world again.
The courting birds
Are chasing love;
The tiny lambs
Play in the field,
And the sleeping earth
Is stirring now;
God's glorious bounty
Is revealed.

V B D'Wit

Seasons - Winter

Hard crust on soil once moist,
Glazed pool, a blue green ice,
Branches suspended with weight of snow,
Upward stretch to meet muted glow,
Long shadows over barn and mill,
Winter covering, the earth stands still.

Then comes spring, her bright green presence,
A new vivid rapture, a transcending radiance,
Dispelling the gloom of dismal days,
Illuminating splendour, daffodils blaze,
Snowdrops, primrose, through new born green,
Changed to landscapes verdant, once barren, lean.

Summer then, long light days,
Everything clear cut, or diamond tipped haze,
The chicks are grown, the corn is high,
Ripples on white flecked waves, sapphire blue sky,
Summer bicycles, holidays far away,
Linger sweet dalliance, go not away.

Autumn follows, a year fulfilled,
Nuts, fruit, squirrels, larder filled,
Swallow and Swift bid us temporary adieu,
Winds rising fitfully, whirling leaves mist the view,
A soft shaded calm then pervades over all,
As warm from our windows, we witness the Fall.

Grace Wade

Springtime

Have you seen all the little buds, a-sprouting on the trees,
have you seen the flowers bursting from the ground,
have you noticed the subtle changes in the leaves upon the tree,
have you seen the wonders happening all around.

It is springtime, it is special, new life starting everywhere,
lambs a-hopping, buds a-popping, God creates with loving care.

Do you marvel at a rosebud, do you wonder at a leaf,
do you see a blade of grass all on its own,
do you see the birds a-flying, way up high into the sky,
do you feel that you are never all alone.

When the sun comes up each morning and it drives away the gloom,
do you see the rays reflected in the stream,
you can see the colours sparkling at the start of this new day,
it must be very real, it's not a dream.

As you look across the meadow, can you see the browns and greens,
can you see the hidden hues that lie beneath,
then you look and see the shadows under trees and bushes too,
as you gaze in silent awe across the heath.

Trevor Rampley

Waiting

Safe, as I wait for the push
The call that will with a gush
Arouse my every sense to a world
Chosen from stars that swirled,
With its water, warmth and light,
For men with the gift of sight.

The warmth that I have known;
The support that I have grown
To expect, ever present ever real,
Is there, but for it I must now feel.
I'll have to wait for my feed
And for the comforting I need.

But now I, upstanding
I Need knowledge and understanding.
With my peers I share my fears
But in the dark my cheeks are wet with tears
Tomorrow when it's light I'll not be late
I'll be first and others will have to wait.

I'll take steps towards another wait
To fit into the system called the State.
In my turn, I will be told
And I will earn applause, or scold
But the time will come or so I read
When I will own my every deed.

On my own two feet I'll have to stand
When I join the Secondary band
There my waiting will begin in earnest
To top the list I must be sternest
Striving my whole life through
To keep abreast or ahead of you and you.

Soon my name will take a shape
Recognition from which there's no escape.
For a status and a place I'll yearn
Credentials of worth I'll have to earn
Some waymarks will have an appointed date
But for the key to the door of life, I must wait.

Unfamiliar ground and its awesome frustration!
The challenge and excitement of competition!
Rewards and satisfaction from achievement!
And success with its contentment!
Doubled at least by simply sharing
Waiting for a partner equally caring.

Having sown I must wait to reap
A responsibility that will not be cheap.
The interim accounts and the dividends I meet
Will help with the winding up of my balance sheet.
I hope to be 'All There' at St Peter's gate
And in His queue, pleased to wait.

Jack Lowe

For Ever And Ever

Of all the wonders of the earth
Nothing surpasses the gift of birth
From minute insect to giraffe tall
All wait for the awakening call
Bringing responsibilities like no other
For animal and human mother
To protect their young with love and care
Be it tiger, elephant or polar bear
Fish swim through many oceans deep
To spawn and their life cycle keep
Birds fly thousands of miles to migrate
And for their destination are never late

Does any being starting life on earth
Ever recall their moment of birth
For most the wonder soon can fade
Forced by life's struggles into the shade
Until a new arrival we see
And think with awe that once was me

Joyce Atkinson

Untitled

Lying beneath a blooming tree,
And gazing with unfocused eyes into heaven
And beyond . . .
The wonder of spring is upon me,
Bringing life from nowhere,
Colour so vividly varied that no copy
Created by man could compare,
Smells that mix and merge together,
Giving the fresh air an added spice,
A wonder so nice, the mind skips and
Dances to inhale!
And arriving at my ears, carried by the
Wind the song of birds is changed and
Livelier still it goes, soft rays of sun
Dance upon my face, as I lie half
Controlled into peaceful emptiness
And grace, gently I drift into a sleepy
State. The magic of spring is here and
Love is in the air.

Jae Willis

By A Creator

Creation yet a mystery. Perhaps
Will always be why time
Or circumstances will not reveal
An history, a fact, or sign.
Amongst the mysteries. We know
That this is really so and in our
Latter day surmise, in time or space
While we can or cannot count the hour
The future is deduced. Where
Beginning, where to end poised
In a universe neither here not there
We cannot perpend. If noised
Abroad. Yet daily while in
Dreams imagined in the season's
Multi-play old or new life
Created without reasons
In a world now called a threat
The joy of being is our debt
To not contend in the affray
To kill our wonder, without regret.

For life takes many forms
We know be it the spirit or
The light in all we see, a
Conceiving not less, in natural lore
While the life we have not
Killed yet friendly smiles upon
Our fate, in this second also given
Forget man's malediction on
The beauties we cannot define,
The simple trust of animals true
The sweeping flowers or gleaming dew
The happiness if in tears known to a few.

John Amsden

A Christ Offering

It was August 5th, a Sunday,
That everyone came to call;
Because that was arranged as the one day
For the Christening of Christopher Paul.

Grandparents came up from the seaside and
One or two others still older,
Miffy and Dorothy Grainger and
Great Uncle and Aunt from East Boldre.

Cousins came too from East Boldre,
Wendy and Benjie and Tim
And, unlike the rest of the family,
Everyone of them slim!

Uncles were there in full measure,
Two fiancees, one genuine Aunt,
Two sisters of our little treasure,
Off-shoots of the same sturdy plant!

Godparents lined up at the front,
Barry and Rene and Mark,
And then they all moved to the font,
Which Christopher thought quite a lark.

Christopher bellowed blue murder
(The Devil reluctant to part!)
While Barry seemed not to have heard a
Sound from him, clutched to his heart!

After the service was over
We all walked along the North Lane.
(And one thing that Chris will discover
He'll never be christened again!)

A toast was proposed and honoured by all,
As we welcomed this young man into the fold.
'Long Life and Happiness, Christopher Paul,
Health and Success, before you are old!'

Patrick Davies

Britspring

Through lime-green
The sun shines tepid.
The sap rises
As the roots spread.
Earth turns over
The shower-loving worms that wriggle up.
Light frosts in the morning
With semi-warmth in the afternoons.
Stirrings in burrows.
Birds find their song.
And the quick step of Man
Turns forward the clock.

David A Chamberlain

Creation

In January there's sometimes snow,
In February spring flowers begin to grow,
March winds bring birds back from sunny climes,
In April birds build nests in oaks and limes,
In May they plant crops of wheat in fields,
In June the wheat ripens to bring forth good
yields,
In July they go for holidays at the beach,
In August the lakes and the mountains they reach,
In September the harvests of fruit mellow,
In October the leaves turn to red, orange and
yellow,
In November the birds fly south in the sky,
In December it's cold and wet or cold and dry.

Susan Mary Robertson

Creation

All the birds of the air, all the fish in the sea,
All the animals that roam the earth,
Were created by God for those of us here,
It's sad that we don't value their worth.
From the largest mammal to the smallest fly,
All have a part to play
In the complex pattern of our existence
As we journey from day to day.
Each blade of grass, every tiny flower,
Each twinkling star in the sky
Are part and parcel of God's creation,
Just as certain as you and I.
We take so much for granted the warmth of the sun, the rain,
We think things are there for the taking,
Free gifts - and yet still we complain.
Night follows day, season follows season,
Each bringing its own sweet reward;
Miracle of miracles, God's hand the provider,
Our Father, Creator, our Lord.
Sometimes we say 'thankyou' for all of His goodness,
But I'm sure we could do a lot more,
All God asks is that we should take care of His world,
That's what He created us for.

Kathleen Poulton

Untitled

Earth was a creation of God
Made many, many years ago
Upon it he put many things
Which we all love so
He made the plants, birds and bees
And helped to make you and me
He gave us eyes, so that we could see
So many beautiful things
But some of us can't see
All that there is upon this earth
And need the help of others
To enjoy Gods wonderful work
So by writing a poem
Or maybe, singing of a song
They too can enjoy the wonders
Like God had planned
No matter what your colour is
Or if you are fat or thin
We are all part of Gods creation
And should be thankful
For all that we have got!

Pauline Haggett

Creation

'It is done, 'He said, taking His repose
On the sixth night: notice the verb
Is not 'finished' but 'done'

Finishing touches were left to those
Who, keeping eyes on the ground
Lifted heads up high
To hear the celestial song
And set their hearts in tune
With His original Thought,
Then called on their human skill
Stretched to the utmost, to fill
In the gaps occasioned
By His Day of Rest.

Mary Frances Mooney

All Creation

Almighty father, Creator
rising triumphant as the day,
full and warm as the summer,
timeless and infinite as eternity.
All is yours.

Almighty God, Redeemer
in the beauty of your creation,
all that is life gives praise,
all of your works pay homage.
All is yours.

Steve Newbury

Did God?

Crouched in my little corner of the garden I gaze in admiration
of nature's glory.
The swallows and butterflies stop to visit me, and the quiet snail
hides beneath a cabbage leaf and I wonder-'What's his
story?'
The green caterpillar comes into her own as she becomes a colourful
butterfly -
'Such a shame that she will live, age and eventually die.

Did God create these lovely specimens?
Women, boys, girls, animals and grand gentle men?
Some short, others tall, some cute, others fat and some slim-
And of course the inner person - not showing hate, love warmth and
coldness - all hidden within?

Mr Toad calls on his sweetheart late evening for a date,
She hurries along not wishing to be late;
The owl in the barn prepares to make flight -
Realising that it's not day but her time- night!

The whistling breezes sing in the stately willow trees,
The swallows are made most welcome there nesting without
paying expensive fees;
A friendly pigeon perches on my shoulder -
I would have held it in my hands had I been bolder.

Did God create these wonderful animals all alone
Fashioned them with love and tenderness while sitting on a smooth
marble like stone?
He breathed life into every one and gave Adam the task of
naming them -
While He remained Master - the Captain at the helm.

David Shields

Creation

Before time had been invented.
Before the wheels turned.
Before the mother's painful gift.
Before the meteor appeared.
Before the sun warmed our world.
Before the bees swarmed around the flowers.
Before the dog slept by the hearth.
God was thinking and imagining.

He created noise out of silence.
He created fun and laughter.
He created cascading water into unknown pools.
Light and shade created contrast.
Freedom of choice between good and evil.
Freedom to love and to hate.
He gave all things to use or abuse.
He gave us the ability to remember or forget.

He gave us His Word to guide us.
He tries to teach us wisdom and discipline.
He tries to create peace and harmony.
He wants us to search for the essential.
He wants us to be Holy.
Where in all creation do we find the children of God?
Where does God's Spirit dwell?
Who acts on His Word?

In this busy fascinating tumult
Who can find the Creator?
Who has found the waters of everlasting life?
Who even wants to find God?
In the chaos and kaleidoscopic ever changing scene
Will we ever stop and think?
Will we ever appreciate and thank our Creator?
Can't we ever love our Father in Heaven?

Barry Broadmeadow

Garden Secret

How do you do it Lord?
Look at the garden
A kaleidoscope of colour,
Shape and texture,
Chameleon shadows
Changing, changing, changing,
How do you do it Lord?
The TV shows asks
'How do they do it'
And someone has an answer.
But your answer Lord is hidden,
Best not to ask.

Elizabeth Gwilliam

My Little Primrose

(For Tegan)

Like the new-born lambs,
it will be born into the spring.
Surrounded by the birds,
so sweetly they will sing.

It starts off a seed,
to fertilise an egg.
Who would think it develops,
to arms, body and legs.

I feel it moving all around,
kicking me inside.
Hic'cupping and jumping,
and going from side to side.

Ten tiny fingers,
ten tiny toe's.
Blonde or dark haired,
no one really knows.

As long as this life
growing here inside,
is healthy and well
happy and alive.

Just like the insects,
birds and the bees.
Bluebells on the riverbanks,
blowing in the breeze.

And when baby Tegan comes,
she will be such a treat.
Just like the springtime primroses,
scent smelling so, so sweet.

Yvonne Tyerman

Heaven On Earth

White beauty of a winter's morning,
Sparkling hoarfrost in the sunlit air,
Trees a-dazzle with snow-tipped fingers -
Heaven is here.

Iced diamonds drip from frosty eaves,
Feather'd patterns on the window glass,
Hedges clothed with lacy cobwebs,
Fox spoor on the grass.

Bare branches in outlined grace,
Rough-barked trunks with shredded snow
Stand against the blue horizon -
Heaven is now.

Frost gives way to softer earth,
The miracle of spring begins.
Nurtured by the gentle showers
New life creeps forth.

Green tipped snowdrops lift their heads,
Turning to the warming sun
That tells all living things on earth
That heaven's begun.

E D Sulston

In The Beginning

This question grips the minds of all the world,
From where did we begin, and when and how?
The question rings throughout the aisles of time.
Intellect and reason seek to answer
While faith accepts what everyman should know
'In the beginning God created Heaven and Earth'.

The swirling mist within the dark of space,
Formless murmuring of a pregnant quiet.
The soul of man still waits in such a place
And seeks to find his purpose in the void,
While darkness hides the face of what will be
Formless prayers are offered up to God.

From somewhere deep within that inner space
There comes the movement of a quiet breath.
This movement once begun will never cease,
The breathe of life, which brings to chaos peace,
Which fills the emptiness with springing life
Laying the blue print of eternity.

The Spirit gave the earth its breath of life,
Laying the fuse that God alone could light.
All these works were hidden in the darkness,
Until God's Voice was heard - 'Let there be light'
Each tiny atom burst into a fire
Which glowed and rose into a shining light.

The mighty wheel of God's creation turning
Sun, moon and stars were set into the skies.
The land and sea, and all that in them are,
While God held out His hands and said 'Amen'
Come ev'ry one and sing a hymn of praise,
For Him who holds the world, still in His Hands.

S Groom

Today's World

Today's world is bold, and grey
Many colours, turn into a gay
World, Inspirations leap to compute
Discard the old - lets loop the loop.
We leap with joy, for we are freed
Idea's blend, there's thrice the need
For we have multitudes to feed

Today's world, where do we go?
To ease the pain, so many know
That they cannot take the pace
Some time the world loses a whole race
Of people, confusion bound, who cannot start
To live again - can we create a new heart?
To propel a nation, that's' science art.

Dorothy Ronald

Nature's Song

See the glory of a sunset sky
Hear a lark's sweet song to cloud on high.
Watch the young lambs in a field at play
Think of beauty each and everyday.
Fill your senses with a flower's perfume
Drink in raindrops, jewels in the gloom.

Feast on nectar from a blossom bright
Honey bees collect for your delight.
Touch a fragile snowflake, icy cold
Nature's loveliness you may behold.
Beauty all around in every tree,
Gracefully a sea bird flying free.

Marvel at the ocean's mighty power
Changing clouds above from hour to hour.
Whispers of a breeze or stormy crash
Thunder's roar, after the lightning flash.
Ripples on the sea shore calm and still
Sunlight peeping over yonder hill.

Soft moonbeams, the starlight all night long.
Snow capped mountain's singing nature's song.
Autumn leaves a'falling, red and gold
Springtime buds and baby chicks to hold.
Buttercups and daisies, meadowlands,
Rivers flowing down to timeless sands.

Volcanic eruptions, fiery force,
Endless seas, the tempest flows a course.
Earthquaking and movement everywhere
Shimmering and shaking, the trees are bare.
As the powers of nature sing their song
Echoing forever to the world belong.

Joan Heybourn

Creations

All things must have beginning, *created* somehow at the start.
Foundation be built very firmly, so it will not fall apart.
Large skein of wool will need winding, add pairs of needles each
size.
Around them a circle of patterns *created* to draw peoples eyes.
Those on their own have no meaning, like that are simply fine sight,
Beautiful in the shop window, *creation* of compact delight.
Bought with intention to use them, they *create* colour and light.
Once those big skeins have been winded into a very large ball,
Still in the fingers of Buyer *creates* coloured clothes from it all.
Car engine has to be switched on, *creating* sound and much steam.
Everything has a beginning, sleep is needed to *create* sweet dream,
A fairy tale world is *created* in minds of small children at play.
Harmonic peace is *created* at bed time to end every day.
Tune brilliantly played on piano, sound *creates* soft harmony,
We listen, there is *created*, magic musical melody.
Created in kitchen cook made us, meals which are fit for a queen.
Colours and tastes so delightful, never ones palate demean.
All items have a beginning, *created* or given birth,
Otherwise could not be used by;- people living on earth.
Words first thing shared by all men, followed by learning life's way.
This forms the pattern of friendship, *created*, meant always to stay.
God took six days to make this world, and on the seventh did rest.
Flowers, seas, skies and good earth, positively in place he felt best.
Adam and Eve put in garden, meant to remain happily,
Serpent however spoiled that plan, tempting in way he could see.
Look on this world and its wonders, marvels in all ways there be.
Creations of Great God almighty, put there for you and for me.

Barbara Goode

God's Creation: An Expression Of Love

God at one time was on His own,
But never did He feel alone.
In every way perfectly complete
With all that's needful was He replete.

Out of His love infinite and great
Upon God there came the urge to create
That He with others His love might share
And spread His love everywhere.

To fill the depths of empty space
Countless galaxies God put in place;
For giving pleasure they were made,
By Him in splendour were all arrayed.

Spirit creatures did He then create,
Angels in their ranks, small and great,
Who allegiance to Him were free to give
And in His love to serve and live.

For this earth He had a special plan:
To bring to birth His creature man.
In a paradise garden He had them placed
And with His likeness were they graced.

Thru God's creation we perceive His might
And in its beauty take delight.
Filled with wonder, overcome by awe
The God we love, we love the more.

John Williams

Icy Fingers

Hedgerows a-sparkle like stars;
Spiders have been weaving again.
Frost has left icy fingers
On its journey down the lane.

Winter grips the barren land:
From nostrils vapour traces.
As they're muffled up in clothes,
One can only see people's faces.

Countryside is *deaf* silent:
Nought to disturb silence is there.
Birds are quiet as the grave;
The fox has gone to his lair.

Slowly mist begins to form,
Rolling o'er hedge and meadow:
Everything is blotted out,
Hidden is the frost and snow.

J Millington

The Oak Tree

For centuries now the mighty oak tree has stood
On a desolate meadow where once was a wood
Your untold beauty you bring especially to me
Not a blot on the landscape like many just see

You had been surrounded by hedgerows, shrubbery and trees
Now all felled by man or died from disease
You've survived all the elements of frost, snow and storm
Your trunk severely weathered and branches all torn

In spring when your buds come forth in the sun
Your forest green coat has just begun
Birds find you a safe haven so they're nesting here
Whilst many grey squirrels from your trunk holes appear

Your foliage clad boughs they spread far and wide
In the summer you shade me and wildlife can hide
As you shed your cupped like fruit of tiny acorn
We hope many more grand oaks may be born

In autumn your elegance you cannot deceive
The colour of deep green has gone from your leaves
As they turn to russet, gold and dark brown
Falling like a paper carpet onto the ground

In winter your outline is like a ghost in the dark
You stand completely naked, your branches so stark
Then with the fall of snow you are draped in white
King of the winter wonderland you grace with delight

Oh tree you are such a wonderful creation
May you continue to be the native of this nation
Not only sanctuary and shelter you give
Because without the tree how would we live?

Linda Brown

The Chestnut Tree

In winter's cold, my branches point bare twigs toward the sky.
My gnarled and horseshoe scarred old trunk, sleeps quiet till spring
is nigh.
When I feel the sap rise through my veins, a stirring in my shoots,
And find grey skies turned tender blue, and Snowdrops round my
roots.

I send out eager sticky buds, that burst forth into green.
Soon blossomed candles, pink and white, stretched skywards will be
seen.
For a week or two, I'll stand in glory, clothed in pink and white,
And hold my candles Heavenward, a truly lovely sight.

But when my blossom falls, like pink confetti on the ground,
My fruits like spiky cannon balls appear, pea green and round.
Then once again I'll feel the chill of autumn in the air,
As ripened Conkers fall to earth, my branches soon to bare.

My yellow fingered leaves point down, where lying on the ground
The glowing burnished Chestnuts lie, their fruits so full and round.
Small boys will fill their pockets, taking home their plundered booty.
How few will stop to pick one up, and marvel at its beauty.

With another cycle over, and a tiredness in my heart,
My rusty leaves will warm the ground, while I sleep through
winter's dark.
Till I feel the Snowdrops stirring, beneath my twisted roots,
And know it's time to waken, and send forth my tender shoots.

Hilda Jones

Thoughts In A Garden

I know I am with my Creator day after day
Whether digging or planting my thoughts often stray
Toward Him and the wondrous things he's provided
My health and my hands so helpfully guided

Without His warm sun and soft heavenly rain
Gentle breezes the dew again and again
My tilling would be quite futile indeed
Without His rich earth the bed for the seed.

What a joy to attend on such a Creation
Then to harvest the fruit in due adoration
To see all the colours of His beautiful flowers
To rest in their fragrance in late evening hours

At the end of the day, my prayer then must be
To awake on the morrow and once again see
All the beauty around on His earth in His sea
My prayer please accept God most humbly from me
It is only you God that can make a fine tree

Fred Norgrove

The Announcement Of Spring

At break of dawn a multicoloured sky
As people in their beds are loathe to wake
Not knowing that a change for good is nigh,
The difference to their lives that this will make
And now the sky dons robes of blue and white
Flowers, so vivid, now opening with great pride
The languid tortoise deigns to appear in sight
And changes, now on view, are far and wide.
On green pleasant hills, important greetings
From brand new life that really do astound,
When budding trees, their shadows cast with feelings
Bringing fresh hope and true joy all around
As on leafy boughs blackbirds will then sing
These fine harbingers of change welcome 'Spring'

Irene Grahame

Lovely Day

In this lovely world to-day
People haven't time to pray
It really cannot be much fun
Living life on the run
No time to stop and look around
No time to see where we are bound
How did we all become so driven?
Surely life was meant for living
Twenty four hours a day were given
Two minutes of this is not a lot
When you think of what we've got
A world of beauty to behold
So come along and let's be bold
Take two minutes just to say
Thank you for this lovely day.

Brenda Norman

The Miracle

'I don't believe in miracles',
You'll hear some people say,
For they believe that those events
Can't happen here, today.

But miracles do happen.
I see them all the time.
I don't mean healing sickness, or
Changing water into wine.

My miracle commences
When I buy a pack of seeds,
And when the time is right for it
And I've cleared away the weeds,
I open up the packet
To reveal what looks like dust,
And plant it in the rich, brown, earth
As every gardener must.

And when I've waited long enough,
A tiny shoot appears.
It grows and grows into a flower
Which blooms for many years.

So here's my little miracle.
How does that tiny crumb
Know it must be Lobelia,
And not Chrysanthemum?

Lilian Hellam

Gifts Galore

This morning I woke and was filled with glee,
The sun was shining on you and me.
It was lighting up that superb blue sky,
Life feels good and we all know why.

The birds are singing to find a mate,
There's joy in the air and we know the date-
The lambs in the field are jumping and skipping,
Spring makes us all feel like laughing and singing.

The daffodils sway in the gentle breeze,
Crocus yellow, purple for the birds to seize.
Snowdrops burst through the hardened earth,
This is a time of gladness, happiness and birth.

God has given us these remarkable things,
The wonders that Spring always brings.
Enriching our lives from day to day,
Helping and guiding us on our way.

But the greatest miracle on this our earth,
Is the child we greet at the phenomenal birth.
Beginning a life in this wondrous world,
Worth more than the treasure of silver or gold.

Dorothy Whitehall

Gentle Stranger

Do you see him standing there
the stranger with the gentle stare
you don't
Well, look again and see
the man who died for you and me
born upon one Christmas day
this gentle man was here to stay
to clean up all of mans decay

Yet for this to be understood
they nailed him to some cruel wood
up high for all the world to see
He hung in pain and misery
giving his life for you and me
what pain he took
yet he gave him not a backward look.

A J Marshall

Tiny Miracles

(Dedicated to Spencer and Jordan Glass
Born 4/3/96 . . . By God's Grace)

Their mother and their dad were shocked when first they knew
They thought there was only one . . . Then, learned that there were . . . two
Thru their mother's months of struggle . . . we all waited for their birth
But . . . much too soon . . . our wait was over. Our babies joined us here on earth

At only one pound four . . . and one pound ten . . . we knew their chances would be grim
We prayed that they could make it, and put all our faith . . . in Him
As those who loved them began the vigil . . . and prayers for God to see them thru
Two tiny boys began a mighty struggle . . . trying to make those prayers . . . come true

We kept hearing they might not stay with us . . . but, all along . . . we knew!
Our boys . . . would not give up their fight . . . and, on and on they grew
We knew . . . God . . . was watching over them. He held them in his hands
As, continued prayers for their survival . . . stretched all across the land

Two precious, tiny angels . . . so fragile . . . and so small
Tho, the odds were all against them . . . they survived . . . to show them all
As the days stretched to weeks . . . then, months . . . our vigil still we held
Thru hurdle after hurdle . . . we kept praying they would be well
On and on . . . against all odds . . . our tiny babies grew

Each day . . . each ounce . . . a milestone . . . a blessing to be praised . . . .
By all of us who love them . . . whose hands toward God . . . were raised
At last . . . we saw two joyful days . . . they'd each go home to mom and dad
Cherished and loved by all of us . . . no greater joy . . . we've had

Their will to live . . . amazes us . . . so tiny . . . yet so strong
We all know they're very special. We've known it all along!
Precious boys, we now believe in miracles. God's shown us that they're true
We'll never doubt, or wonder . . . for, our miracles . . . are . . . you!

Mary Beth Bott

Creation

On the first day God created the earth,
Blessed it with life form
And he was well pleased.

On the second day God created virtues,
Chose them carefully
And scattered them
Upon the earth.

On the third day God created man
In his own image
But man needed companionship
So God created woman.

On the fourth day God created love
'Love one another' he said
But love alone was not enough
And was lacking.

On the fifth day God created trust
'Trust one another' he said
Without trust
Love would not flourish.

On the sixth day God created understanding,
But found it necessary
To create another emotion
Which could work thoughout the world.

On the seventh day God created forgiveness.
By creating forgiveness
Love, Trust and Understanding
Had played their part.

Betty M Varley

God's Small Miracles

A butterfly's wing,
A gossamer string,
An angel singing a lullaby.
A baby's cry,
A kittens sneeze,
A leaf floating by on a soft summer breeze.

A dew kissed rose,
Sand on your toes,
A meadow golden with corn.
A velvet dawn,
A cloudy sky,
A bird as it learns how to fly.

Pauline Chambers

Leaves

All sorts of patterns to see,
Shades of green varying with one another.
What about the Ivy? with a serrated edge,
The different shades of green mingling together.
Dragonflies are hovering over the lily pads.
Out comes a frog and sits on a great leaf,
When a shower comes
Some leaves hold the dews for the insects.
Then the upright sword of the lily
And also the daffodil leaf so narrow.
Sunlight dapples through the leaves,
Of all the different trees
Sun warms the ground for the plants.
So out comes all the little leaves
Followed by the flowers.
All the different colours
Mingling together over Gods earth.
The velvety leaf of an African Violet
Prickly holly leaves, with red berries
And shimmering green leaves.
The spiky needles of a fir tree,
Drooping leaves of a carnivorous plant
Golden leaves in autumn.
Different shades in all their glory.
Falling to the earth to enrich the soil.
But Hey Presto! the next spring
Little buds appear everywhere!
Yes! The leaves have a glory all of their own

Margaret Pearce

Creation Speaks

I went with a friend on an out-of-door retreat on the
borders of Dartmoor at a time, when a catalogue of disasters
and broken relationships had caused her to have a physical
and mental breakdown. Every day, we were taken for a
long walk to a prearranged spot and given a view on which
to meditate. All was fine, whilst the weather held, but
one day, the heavens opened, as only they can on Dartmoor
we battled against the rain, driven by loud, bleak winds to
Scorhill Stone Circle.
As we neared this site of ancient stones, it loomed
eerily against the sombre moorland horizon. Veiled in mist,
the moor gave a remote and frightening appearance.
Completely forsaken, except for some shaggy-coated wild ponies
grazing nearby, sad and fearful thoughts sprang into our minds.
'We must be mad', we said consolingly to each other, my friend
talked about her life; desolate, lonely and empty, like the
still, silent and rugged valley all around us. Then, quite
unexpectedly, we caught sight of a solitary sundew
flower, rising out of the blackness of the moorland
bog; its fragile beauty giving us hope in the midst
of this barren wasteland. Suddenly, we were both
visualising how the moor would look if flowers bloomed
over its undulating ground.
God had met us in these ancient and ruined surroundings
and revealed the beauty and richness, which exists even
in the most depressing of situations.
God had waited for us at this place of dereliction
and death and removed the mists from before our eyes,
as Jesus had done for Mary, as she wept outside the
empty tomb. He had called our names and dried our tears,
so we could return home joyfully, eager to share the
good news with others in their desolation and despair,
'He is risen; He is risen indeed,' Thanks be to God, Amen.

Brenda Ford

Joys Of Spring

Oh! what joys we encounter in spring
When the pretty bluebells
Nod their heads and ring
Their bells in the fairy dells,
        forests and meadowland.

Squirrels are searching for their nuts
Hedgehogs wake up from their resting
                quarters
Rabbits and hares waltz in
                the spring
Vaults of merriment over the
                rivulet waters

Trees are wanting to open their new
                green leaves
When the spring sunshine covers
                them
And the gentle breeze believes
They will take heed and signal
                a spring theme

Bees are busy working hard for
                their queen
Her nursery cells full to the brim
                with young babies,
They are so full of life and keen
To be of service to young flowers
                they see.

Butterflies and moths in their
                homespun shelters
Begin to come to life and seek
        the wonders of meadows and lake
A slow progress but never the less
Welters of wanton swaying, the
        new insects this movement they can
                take.

Thoughts of birds coming home from
abroad
Flying in thousands on the wing
Crowds of mothers and babies
Brood of merry breath taking
chatterings

Earth worms making love to
fashion the soil
Bringing to life the vegetable and
flower seeds
Great expectations to toil
To make their food tasty and
do excellent deeds.

The grass is at its best
That heavenly green not known at
other times
Straight as a dye no pest
To ruffle its merry chimes.

Human beings begin to feel the
presence of spring
All things around them steer
Sunshine and showers are joyous
reminders
Of the finishing with many a cheer
that winter is behind us.

Oh! what joy can be each spring
When laughter and life has become
gloriously happy
There's no time like the ring and
Ding-a-ling of yappy springtime.

Alma Montgomery Frank

Spring Banners

Arise! Awaken, sleepy snowdrops.
Pure and bright, white banners blow.
Frost has lost its iron mantle.
Silver sunbeams soften snow.

Shimmer, shining aconites.
Sweet coverlets of gold, abound.
Small sensation - God's creation
Springs eternal, all around.

Burst, brown buds on barren branches.
Dress - your fresh, green garment grows
Fast and fleeting, winter cheating,
Flutter, leafy furbelows.

Blossom, bluebells, subtly stirring.
Pierce the earth, revived, restored,
Rooted deep in secret places,
Richly nurtured by the Lord.

Pauline Pullan

The Crucial Six Days - Mirablile Dictu!

Have you ever pondered over what you might have been today,
Had not God made the crucial six days - Monday to Saturday?
Had not God's spirit, hovering over the void disarray,
Ordered Light, creating the day and the night, on the first day?
Had not God ordered a firmament, dividing the waters,
Creating Heaven on day two - Morning that evening alters?
Had not God gathered the dry land together calling it earth,
Filling it with grass, herbs, and fruit yielding trees on day the third?
Had not God set greater light by day and lesser lights by night
In the firmament on day four - so, the seasons to divide?
Had not God created seas abounding with living creatures,
And birds that fly across the firmament on dies quintus?
Had not God made the beast of the earth, cattle and creeping thing,
Creating Adam and Eve on day six, all else transcending?
Had not these six days of miracles of creation occurred,
Humanity may still be nebular atoms and neuted,
Sans form or substance, void and dark on the face of the very deep
The miracle of God's handiwork was marvellous indeed!
The most exquisite Garden of Eden, He planted eastward,
A mist from the earth, to water the whole garden, He ordered;
The glorious dawn, and the gorgeous sunset, the star-studded sky,
The awesome waterfalls, and the radiant rainbow, to espy;
The snow-capped mountains, the glaciers, and the parched, arid deserts,
The coral reefs, the blue sky, the monsoon, and the Rain Forests,
The birds of Paradise, the Robin, plumed peacock, the dancer,
The spotted deer, the lordly lion, the majestic tiger!
God's manifestations are all around from eternity,
Yet, Not One has seen God with the naked eye, positively:
It's all because of Adam's sin at creation, - definitely!
God ordained that humans commune with Him only spiritually,
Though unseen, and omnipotent, He is with us assuredly,
With Grace, unfailing sympathy, undying love - all Profusely!

Welch Jeyaraj Balasingam

We Are All In The Making, We Are All God's Creation

The lamb that leaps,
its tail a flying,
the horse that whinnies,
its spring he's crying.

The sun shines down,
it sparkles off the dew,
the spring is here,
life begins a new.

The grass is cut,
fresh and green,
the calf is born,
both limber and lean.

Shoots pop up,
flowers in bloom,
dogs and cats,
smile up to the moon.

Foxes are creeping,
through distant bushes,
while birds are peeping,
out of the rushes.

God shows his love,
in all his creation,
from ant to elephant,
we are Gods own nation.

Siobhan O'Conchubhair

God's Creation

God's creation is all around us
If we take the time to look
He created this world we live in
A world like an open book
He appears in every flower that blooms
Beside each babbling brook
At the trilling song of a bird
That rises melodic and sweet
He is there on a sunny spring morning
Also at the daybreak's dawning
In the scent of blossoms that bloom
Cheering us from sadness and gloom
God's creation is all around us
If we spare the time to look
Life goes by with bustle and haste
For those seeking, fame and glamour
In a clatter of noise and clamour
So easy to miss His tender touch
The perfect peace, the simple life
Listen to his voice each day
From it help is on the way
His patience all enduring
A hidden substance there to grasp
If only we would heed it
Listen and life takes on new meaning
Stop rushing around filling every hour
Afraid to face His beauty
Life is meant to be a joy an inspiration
Do not let it slip away, in the wrong direction
So many blessings fill our day
There for us to receive them
The warmth of friendship
The laugh of a child
His spirit and love are sent to inspire
To enjoy this world He created
Look around and offer a prayer of thanks
For it is so often belated.

Kathleen Glover

Restart

Soon now the snow will melt
snowdrops and aconite's are here.
Then rain and sleet will pelt
and trees their buds will bear.

Standing tall on slender stems
the daffodils will nod good morn.
This sets the springtime theme
with daisies dancing on the lawn.

Ferns unfold their delicate fronds
birds sing busily at their nests.
Dragonflies dart across the pond
as ladybirds gobble up the pests.

A time of year, with much to do.
Trimming the grass with the old half-moon
sowing and planting, cleaning too.
Then it's summer. Oh! So soon.

J Williams

The Restless Sea

'Neath the waters of the tumultuous ocean
Where adventurous divers show their skill
Of searching the natural waters bed
For exotic creatures that are never still.

There lies a natural world of wonder
Which the ocean covers unceasingly
Despite the boats that amble on
Churning up the waters intermittently

God's creatures roam this wonderland
A tidal sea of nature's creations
Yet sometimes rough and billows roar
Floundering over rocks and crustaceans.

Oh! changes that will never cease
Peculiar to the land and sea
With dolphins leaping over surfy waves
In gladsome days of being free.

When skies are blue there's calmness
But life beneath the waters carry on
'Neath the surging swell of motion
The vertebrates continue living long.

From shore to shore there's miracles
Which we cannot apprehend
For God in all his wisdom
Bestow his mysteries that has no end.

Eileen Chamberlain

My Wonderful Land

As far as the eye can see, reds, yellows and greens,
All across my prairie they can be seen,
But soon the angry winds will come,
Turning my wonderful prairie into dust.

The angry winds blows mother earth across the plains,
Soon the water will be gone, the grass no-more,
As the relentless heat from the scorching sun,
Turns this wonderful prairie into dust.

The dark skies are coming, let them pass me over,
Grey skies overhead, the storm is near,
Soon the rain will wash away the colour of the plain,
Then this wonderful land will be no-more.

Will this terrible weather never abate,
Soon the whistling wind will blight the country side,
Before the whirling tunnel of the terrible tornado
As it roars across my wonderful land.

Violently the rains came, from the darkening sky,
The sky blackened to the fullness of the rain,
As the howling wind and rain blows across the plain,
Electric storm flashers, dancing across the sky.

The sun is brightening now, the sun is out,
The wind and rain has come and gone,
The prairie will recover from it's ordeal,
For come rain or shine, this wonderful land is mine!

Barry Cregg

The Thread

Roseate dawn of soft pink sounds,
this is where first life abounds.
Rivers of milk the opals of life,
the fountainhead stems from the wife.
Slowly days flicker by,
just sleep at first is all that's nigh.
The delicate skin and eyes of blue,
grown soft and plump as days accrue.
Innocence and laughing steps,
stumbling at first then slowly gets
assured and firm even start to run,
well life can be such fun!
Perfect clay in potters hands
moulded in a certain way,
personalities like grains of sand
once shaped by the potter here to stay!
The heady heights and gloomy depths,
maturity with wobbling steps.
Until one day a man full grown
proudly escorts his new wife home.
Once more the thread to start again,
creation of life, mankind's domain.

Ann Ebbs

Gifts Of Grace

Dear Father, when you first created this universe
there was only a dark, waterfilled 'Abyss'
then lights came down from your firmament so wondrous,
causing vegetation, which the rain kept green.
Sky and land became studded with brilliant gems of fantastic colours.
Enhancing the Earth with a profusion of wild life, birdsong and
fragrant flowers
what a wonderful story of artistry can be told
of how God in his Love fashioned and clothed our fantastic bodies,
offering us a share in the creation of mankind and this world!
Yet, so often now, man's greed and selfish behaviour
destroys or refuses these gifts of grace from
our Risen Saviour.

Mary Brechemier

Snow

The wonder of it - the silent surprise;
The whiteness, the brightness beneath
leaden skies;
The clean virginity, delicate symmetry
of snow!

The silence of it - the soft, sudden fall;
The swirling and twirling, the touch
of it all;
The magical, tragical chaos, the coldness
of snow!

It came silently - we were started,
alarmed;
The car wouldn't start! No time to
be charmed!
The mess and distress, the sheer nastiness
of snow!

B R Winbolt

Springtime

Birds sing in the early morning light
Air crisp and clear as the sun breaks through
Carpets of snowdrops everywhere
Magnificent the crocus too,
In every shade of colour and hue,
Sparkling with drops of dew.
Daffodils nodding in the breeze.
Water rippling down the stream.
Wading birds splash and preen
Hares, shadow boxing in the fields.
Calling bleat of new born lambs.
These sights and sounds all there,
As we feel 'Springtime', in the air.

Sheila A Waterhouse

A Precious Gift

I'd say to a man for whom Fatherhood's pending,
It won't be a dawdle, there's no use pretending.
There'll be sleepless nights which at times seem unending.
Hang in there!

This strange little person's dependent on you.
At times you will say, "what the hell do I do?"
But with God in your corner you will see it through-
Believe me!

Old wives' tales abound, and they scarce ever vary.
If taken on board they can really be scary,
But they're only stories to trap the unwary-
Ignore 'em!

Keep looking ahead to this happy event
With hope and excitement the way it was meant,
Then enjoy and cherish this gift heaven-sent-
You'll love it!

Dorothy White

Our Planet Home The Silent War

It's war.
Day and night unseen forces
Strain and vie to overcome.
Silently a quiet army
Plots and plans from many a home.

All intent to gain advantage
In which ever field they strive.
Church and State will soon be gone
But they intend to stay alive.

Undercover silent working.
Day and night ongoing war.
To and fro the battle rages,
Yet life continues as before.

Papers scanned and then discarded.
Headlines noticed by the few.
By the many disregarded.
The only question is 'What's new?'

Fists are clenched and vows are made.
Blood runs hot with passions high.
All this without a sound being heard.
'But you'll agree or you will die'.

Nature too, a great invader
Creeps upon us unobserved.
Man with puny strength strikes back,
The days seem calm and undisturbed.

But soon in pain and desperation
Man will regard his fractured world.
Will look upon the devastation
With the flag of death unfurled.

He'll be circumnavigated.
Soon he will be overcome.
He'll be trampled underfoot.
He will loose his planet home.

In squalor, filth and degradation,
Corrupt and drugg⌈d murderers roam.
Silent forces now victorious,
Man has lost his planet home.

Peter Manson-Herrod

Life

Do not grieve for me,
for truly I did survive.
The body maybe cold and lifeless,
but it was never really alive.
For I am life, independent from the body,
it was merely a vehicle for me.
Manifesting in space and time,
so I needed eyes to see.
But a blind man is still alive
even though he cannot see,
which proves I can survive without sight,
but eyes cannot function without me!
Nor do I need a tongue to exist,
though I did need it to talk.
And I can endure without legs,
they just helped me to walk.
Look at those organs and limbs now though,
absolutely useless without me.
In comparison the body's similar to a toy doll,
which can do nothing without a battery.
I am not bones, blood or brain either,
I exist without any of these.
Of course they serve a purpose,
but isn't life in flowers and trees?
Do they not live without brains or blood?
I animate every form of life you can name.
I repeat, I am the one that brings life,
and all life's one and the same.
Nor am I the cells that form the body,
which is hard to believe I know,
but not one body cell exists today
that existed seven years ago.
Yet I endure unchanged and undiminished,
an immortal, universal flame.
Unaffected by disease, war or famine,
always and forever the same.

For I am eternal, indestructible.
I can never cease to be.
I am the life within all living things.
Do not grieve for me.

Colin Winfield

Untitled

I found Heavens Gate today.
As winds ruffled my hair;
And thought that if you died to this,
I wouldn't really care.
I looked across mountains tops,
As a Supreme Highness would;
And pushed the clouds out of my face,
I never thought I could.
I shook hands with Him then,
He asked me how I felt;
I said 'Oh so much better now,
after all the pain you've dealt'.
I found the answer then,
Listened to Him who knows;
And I could justify everything,
And my sudden awakening shows.

J Miller

By The Thames At Sunset

Way down in the shadow of the west
that wondrous glow of deep vermilion
and orange tint I see;
the gentle stream with a rippling beam
has flown so many years past shaggy isles
with curving banks; to me
it seems like a joyous haven of rest
lost to a world of thankless men.

Harriette Lewis

To Creation

When creation blows her glimmering trumpet,
Fair summer, rich with bountiful display,
And azure skies, heralds splendour:
For among jewel-like scenes and gold veined flight,
The white petalled water lilies float in bright sunlight.
Gaily, magical wings with iridescent glow,
Flitter past the golden wings,
Of glittering dragonflies,
Shimmering below.
And beautiful amber, gauze and silver wings,
Dart and circle through an aerial realm;
And whizzing with flight's droning sound,
Whirl past the shady elm.

Now drowsily, the large furry bee,
Disappears into summer's white bell,
Hovering and humming,
In fragrant flowers to dwell:
Yet too busy, packing pollen baskets
On hind legs, to rest,
She is the dweller of flowers,
And is frequently their guest.
But when the lovely blooms from,
A 'garland dream',
Have perfumed the air,
Through a festooned sheen,
All Nature's wealth shall abundantly flow,
With the magnificence of Nature,
And the splendour of her show.

Christine Hare

Season's Symphonies

Summer slips quietly into autumn -
melancholy days of gold and brown.
Rosehips and blackberries blanket hedgerows.
Farmers' furrows have gouged the ground.
Morning mists on dew drenched meadows -
Cobwebs cling as filigree lace.
Owls screech their protest to silvery moonlight -
Swallows fly southwards - ribbons in space.
Chill breezes rustle the leaves that have fallen from
trees standing sentinel, barren and bare.
Icicles glisten in pale winter sunlight like cascading
crystals suspended in air.
Soon cruel winds over snow swept carpets will herald
the winter with gusts of contempt.
Rivers lie captured in sullen silence -
grey and still, their banks unkempt.
The countryside slumbers in sweet anticipation as
over the crisp air church bells ring.
God is preparing his never ending miracle.
Soon it will be spring.

Elsie Francis

Two's Company Three's A Family

Oh how silently you crept into my life
and settled yourself down,
deep within the very fibre of my being.
There, in that secret place,
God began to knit you together,
and on that chill wintry morn,
I knew nothing of the miracle that was taking place.
Soon I learnt of your existence
and we two spent those next months
in close communion, I can tell you.
Back to back and head to rib,
till you were forced to turn around
and get your head down
into its proper place!
I watched your antics through a belly's wall
and my ever expanding girth.
I planned, prepared in every way
for your forthcoming birth.
I sang to you and dreamed of you,
you'd taken over my life completely.
Each numbered week passed by,
until your appointed hour had come.
On D Day, Delivery Day,
you presented yourself for us to see, to meet at last!
Now your Dad and me, we two became three,
and of course we were - a family.

Jenny Elton

Eden

To see each flow'r, to feel each leaf as first
to spring in Eden; hear the firestart burst
of cracking gorse-pods; read on noon-white skies
the swift inscribe superlatives - she flies
the dance divine; inhale, once stale, in storm
restored, the wind of God from ev'ry form
in firmament and earth; to treat each brute,
mundane or mean, as music from His flute
and view each man as Mother's son, her dream
fulfilled, her fruit, her dear delight, her theme
complete; thus will His will, his pow'r find birth,
His glory and His kingdom come on earth.

Chris Moat

Just A Thought

Some of us are so lucky to enjoy good health
When there are many of those who don't
We can walk, talk, see, hear, smell, work
and play
There are many of those who won't
Young and old alike, those who are terminally ill
And with a variety of afflictions our hospitals
they fill
How must they feel when they see those of us fit
and well
What goes on in their minds, none of us can tell
Class makes no distinction, rich or poor alike
Should not we just spare a thought and be ever
Grateful ill health does not mar our life?
We take our good fortune for granted
Plan for tomorrow without a thought
We never think there may not be a tomorrow
Good health and a long life cannot be bought
Never leave till tomorrow what can be done today
Just a thought for those without choice
either way
If there is a problem in your life
which causes concern
Lady luck may shine your way again and
Jut a thought, your good health she may return

Daisy Helen Thompson

Isabella Plantation: God's Glory Glimpsed

I waft down your endless garden paths,
'Midst mounds of shimmering azalea wings,
'Tween pink and yellow God-breathed flower clouds,
Rolling rainbow concert of Chopin rhythms.

Countless radiant rhododendron angels choir His praise.
Ten thousand thousand tiny royal gold and crimson
Trumpets herald His presence.
Jewel mirrors blaze His glory.
Christ's life and light beam out,
His fire igniting leaf and bud.

Arching azalea Maypole branches
Adorned with bridesmaid chiffon, silk and satin.
Majestic flower-gowned ladies in waiting,
Wedding white 'n pink, their lamps brightly burning,
Await our glorious Groom's appearing.
Sun, moons, stars, flower - Heaven and earth all bloom His glory.

In this gifted moment,
Hummingbird blossoms brush thought aside.
Mind parts for creation's song of
Son-won azalea-rhododendron life.
Upon this estate, extravagant beauty, nurtured, thrives;
God's handiwork banners forth His redeeming grace.

My Lord leads me down His plantation paths,
His grander scheme to show.
He whispers to me as I follow,
'Beloved, these glorious gleamings are but sweet scented shadows.
The Lamb's light filtered, flickering, faint.
But in His triumphal hour, Glory all darkness shatters.
And all the earth with garden grandeur
In Glory covered everymore shall be.'

Beside His shining on the dappled way, I follow,
His wonders dreaming,
'Til sudden sadness deep within me rises.
To think you might not come,
Oh, come away with us -
For, he beckons,
His glory not to glimpse
But eternally behold.

Nina Helene

The Four Seasons

Spring is the time of year everything comes alive
Grass grows again and people thrive
The countryside becomes an amazing scene
As animals roam and once again leaves are green
The time of year when flowers blossom
The coming of spring is really awesome

After spring comes summertime
The season with the most sunshine
When everyone seems to move outdoors
To bask in its glory as the temperature soars
When it turns to evening time outside it's still light
The season of summer is an amazing sight

The season of autumn comes next
It's flowers and trees it mostly affects
The third season that blows an autumn breeze
When the leaves turn brown then fall from the trees
Fallen leaves that litter the local park
When bright summer nights start turning to dark

Then comes winter when nights turn to black
The forth season starts when the clocks go back
It's bitter gales and the howling noise it makes
The time of the year we see the first snow flakes
Through the dark nights the moon shines crystal clear
It's also the season of goodwill and cheer

The making of the seasons was God's, he was the creator
He gave us the 4 seasons to see all the different aspects of nature
With every season he brought something new
He hopes we appreciate the four seasons too.

Neil McClafferty

First Impressions

When first you see a snowdrop
Poke through the frozen earth,
Are you aware that spring is near?
The time of Nature's birth.

Then, when you see a crocus
With fat buds, yellow bright,
You almost know that spring is here
With sunshine's golden light.

Then she arrives in splendour
With flowers in her hair,
With Earth's new growth around her,
The trees no longer bare.

The Earth made new in springtime
Mother Nature at her best,
Each bud by God created
And thus all life is blessed.

Norma Christina Robson

Taraxacum Officinale

No surprise to find abundance
of common yellow dandelion,
companion to the trodden daisy,
heady clover white and purple,
gold-reflecting buttercups,
thistles tall with piercing spikes,
plantain for games of 'chop my head off'-

But *this* one was 'Taraxacum':

Gold and green and . . . tidy!
each leaf rising from the root,
each flowerhead a proud
shining beacon in long grass,
bracts in circles, back to back,
one a clasping green neck-ruffle,
other curved towards hollow stem.

Climb the Alps for edelweiss,
seek hart's tongue fern in Burren grikes,
I choose the treasure in the field beside my house,
no crowd nor cloud of rarest orchid
can dim the glowing beauty of that symmetry,
the colonnade of stems that hold
petalled reflections of the sun.

Once just a weed
today become
Taraxacum.

Oonagh Twomey

The Perfect Wait

I feel so helpless, so out of control,
A life within, developing, growing,
A life that is already loved
And yet nothing I can do to protect it.

The hours and minutes tick by,
Slowly, endlessly,
Full of dreams and plans
But always shadowed by fears.

One day you'll know how precious your life was,
The promise of happiness,
A future,
The joining of two lives
To form a perfect one.

Sleep safely, sleep.

W Stanbury

Singing

Country fields are singing
As crops ripen to a full harvest;
Meadows are bringing forth wild flowers
As the sun shines at Nature's behest.

Woodland glades are singing
As streams murmur and brooks flow;
Scented petals are mingling their fragrances
As gently falling rains feed crystal fountains aglow.

All the birds are singing
As trees come into leaf;
Fresh buds are springing from sap-filled boughs
As winter, long forgotten, comes to grief.

All Nature is singing
As bees hum and hornets drone;
Every insect is winging its way
Towards a destination known or unknown.

The very soil is singing
As buds blossom and seedlings sprout;
All the flowers are tingling with vibrancy
As their trembling petals open out.

Earth's great globe is singing
As flora's panoply begins to shoot;
Vast forests are clinging to steep slopes
As burgeoning blooms, new-born, take root.

All the stars are singing
In myriad orbs of shining light;
Galaxies are flinging their spiral arms heavenward
As golden constellations, showering, grow bright.

The very firmament is singing
As countless fires, like jewels, flame forth;
Heaven's vaults themselves are ringing with glad tidings
From west to east, from south to north.

All Creation is singing
To One who sits upon His sapphire throne.
All bow down and worship Him
As angels themselves, in adoration, lie prone.

One day humankind will be singing,
When Love from on high will end all strife;
And then Creation, in harmony, will join
As one to worship the Lord of life.

Robert D Hayward

Sunset

I stood this evening in the sunset's fiery glow
And bathed in its warm gold light
I felt it was shining just for me
And every plant and flower and tree
As it dipped towards the ascending night
At my feet wild flowers in abundance grew
Sweet tiny blue violets, mauve tipped grasses
Yellow buttercups and pink clover too
And late white hawthorn was also in view
It was a wonderful moment with nature at its best
It was what gives us joy and life its zest
The only sounds were the song of the birds
As they prepared for night to fall
And in a wood across the fields
A cuckoo repeated its loud persistent call
The red sun fell swiftly behind the hill
Highlighting the trees on its crest
This was nature so beautiful
Nature at its very best

Barbara Anne Smith

The Ela[1] *tion Of Creati*[2] *on*

The elation of creation
Is the beauty of the earth
The flowers sweet formation
And the joy of giving birth
The stars that brighten up the sky
The ever flowing sea
What joy beholds the human eye
I'm sure you would agree.

He's crafted every blade of grass
Each branch upon the tree
The land He's formed, the sky He's cast
And the beast that roams so free
In humble admiration
Before my God I'll stand
The elation of creation
Was crafted by His hand.

*[1] Elation
*[2] Creation

David John Dunbar

The Snows Of Spring

Softness, Quietness, Lightness,
Springs white blanket spread
In glistening whiteness
Over hill and dale
Daffodils weary and frail, sagging listless
With springs white burden of frozen hail.

Blackbirds chirp through the garden
In search for worm or seed
Black feathers, yellow beak
Stark contrast to white carpet
Lying beneath their feet
Spring lambs undaunted by the chill
Skipping, playing, bounding over,
Over the snow capped hill.

Shimmering, glimmering, whiteness
Glistening in the sun
Stark contrast to an ever darkening world
Changing seasons what joy or sorrow they bring
Pass away like the snow,
The snows of spring

Frances Gibson

The Creator

He, the greatest artist that ever lived,
Who's mighty mind created us,
And being made from nought but dust
Yet being thus are not elide.
Set each amid surrounding fair,
Gave each a soul as heavenly gift,
Which to His side at last might lift,
Each single life into His care.

Set first of all His canvas there, containing all that we would need.
And then, His waiting brush he freed, creating man as His first care.
Set Him as Lord of all the earth, to rule as overseer there.
Gave fruitfulness, that all should bear in plenitude with each new birth

That man might rest his human frame, He gave him night with darkness shod
Then, with an understanding nod, He shook His brush and soon there came
Myriad's of twinkling stars across the sky, another stroke dipped in soft light
And the moon became Queen of night, so show us still that God is nigh.

With day He took away nights cloak, so we might see the wonders of the world,
Which with each moment are unfurled, and, knowing man, set high his hopes,
That even in the humblest mind, His handiwork shows through
In every kindly act we do, which upon life's path we find.

He clothed the world in loveliest shades
From darkest brown and deepest green.
And where before brown earth had been,
Soon were showing the tiny blades,
Of new born plants, which He did give
To fulfil their purpose here,
Each breathing thing has nought to fear,
For He gave His Son that we might live.

And in the giving surpassed all heights
Which human man can hope to do,
But to His creed we can be true,
And give to everyone their rights
For God who made us, understands
Each one of us, and loves us all,
And even if at times we fall,
We still are safe in His outstretched hands

Dorothy Ventris

All Seasons Have A Message

Winter is here; the branches of deciduous trees are bare.
Frost rimes the grass and coats the slated roof.
Gardens look sad, bereft of annual flowers once so fair:
Freeze stiffened icicles hang spiky and aloof.

But beauty still abounds, the wintry sun lights up the frosted bark,
Bringing sweet hope of newly swelling buds in early spring.
It will endure the frost, the ice, the snow, the early dark;
Life will stir again for loveliness is born from suffering.

None can hold back the spring save He who created earth and heaven.
Season will follow season to give their flowers, fruits and seeds.
He holds the key to the promise He made to us His leaven,
He loves and cares for us, a Father knows His children's needs.

Winter must abide a while and be endured for spring to rise again;
Summer will surely follow, bringing warmth and colour to long carefree days.
Autumn effects the fall, a cycle of seasons, a constant refrain;
The magic of each unfolding brings the blessings and the praise.

Doreen Barwell

The Gift

Sunday morning, gardening time,
Another chance to see
The wonders that the Lord created
Just for you and me.

The dowdy caterpillar,
Not the prettiest of things,
Will soon become a butterfly
With lacy, velvet wings.

And there, a spider swinging
On a silken silver thread,
Prepares to weave its magic
'Twixt a fence post and the shed.

Kaleidoscopes of colour,
That not long ago were seeds,
Reds, and blues, and here and there
A scattering of weeds.

An apple tree, now in full bloom,
A breeze that gently blows,
And morning dew that glistens
Like teardrops on a rose.

The tapestry of nature
Is once again unfurled,
And once again I thank the Lord
For giving us this world.

K White

Cat

I love thee, O Cat,
For achieving unity between the realities and the trivialities
of life; for retaining regality when discovered indulging
in a fish-entangled dream of cream with whisker-twitching
anticipation.
I love thee, O Cat.
For the height of the lithe lightness that leaps to the
inconsequential feather; for the depth of the deep contemplation
that muses on the hidden truth buried in the huge universe;
for the breadth of the untouchable serenity of feline peace.
I love thee, O Cat,
For thy perfection in a world imperfect which makes thee not a
lover but Love, not a hunter but Fate, not a killer but Death
itself.
Because I have loved with Love and fought with Fate and am
doomed to Death,
I love thee, O Cat.

Catherine Gregory

Freedom

Ah! To be a bird so free,
To fly with ease from tree to tree,
Weary limbs a burden gone,
And heavy, gasping breathing done.
Worry is some unknown thing,
And happiness a song to sing.
Riches great he'll never need
He has the sun and food to feed.
Moon and stars companions bright
He has no need of candlelight.
Sailing wings outspread on breeze,
His music flows from whispering trees.
No one thinks, to hear his song,
What words he lets slip from his tongue.
Words of freedom, words of love
For sun and moon and stars above.
Words that tell of lovely sights
That he has seen on his lone flights.
Love of breezes, leaves and trees
And every little thing he sees.
Love to God does he express
In his very happiness.

Pauline Dodworth

Creation

The earth was nothing - formless and empty
The surface clothed in darkness
The Spirit of God was hovering
Over waters that were lifeless

With one powerful breath, God did speak
He said 'Let there be light'
So darkness and light did separate
Light became day, darkness night

God then said, 'An expanse let there be'
So the waters did divide
The expanse became sky, the waters sea
And land came from ground that had dried

Then God did speak once again
'Let the land produce vegetation'
So plants and trees and seeds and fruits
Became part of His creation

God then placed in the expanse of sky
Lights to guide and lead
Sun and moon and planets and stars
To mark seasons, days and years

The seas then filled with living things
The sky then filled with birds
God blessed them all and said to each
Be fruitful throughout the earth

'According to their kinds, produce living things'
God then told the land
'Livestock, creatures, wild animals
To move along the ground'

Then God said, 'Let us make man'
And make them in our image
So they can rule over all the earth
And dominion to them we'll give

God then looked at His creation
It was good all that He'd made
And there was evening and there was morning
The end of the sixth day

Finally, in all their vast array
The Heavens and Earth were completed
God finished the work he'd been doing
And on the seventh day He rested

Mandy Harvey

Summer

From high on hill the halo'd spires
Unto the balmy heavens dwell.
And through the rising, dough-like air
Cuts the tolling parish bell.

Drenched by torrents from a swollen sun
Impaled by her fork-like rays.
Exposed, the hard-baked soil doth split
Neath the smouldering haze.

A butterfly drifts on the gentle breeze
O'er the shimmering fields of hay.
And in lush meadows the children craft
Buttercup and daisy-chains.

O'er the moonlit, silhouetted lake
A million fire flies dance.
And a vixen tears a fly-blown corpse
Under the owl's hypnotic trance.

Oh sweet summer you radiate such warmth
As you wave your magic wand.
Like the swan that majestically doth glide
O'er the glassy, tranquil pond.

A R Frape

Seasonal Changes

The bleating of the lambs - the mooing of the cows,
relating to all that spring has come -
Apple, - pear, - plum - bloom 'tis sweet,
aye, more fragrant than the rum.

Summer brings the sweltering heat,
when one can work hard and long -
Then family life can become so irksome,
the way that affects even the strong.

Chestnuts, leaves of red, gold and brown -
Shortening days - clocks back one hour,
remind us that autumn is here -
just where was that former leafy bower?

Winter's a time for reflection,
upon what's been both done and seen -
For a-midst the winds, the frost, and the snow,
we all prepare for what's not yet been.

The seasons come and the seasons go,
but we'll go on forever -
For we all are spiritually endowed-
and our souls won't die-no, never.

Kevin McCann

Surrounded By His Love

There are many ways in which God is known to
us, one is through nature.
Look around at the wonderful and beautiful things
made by our loving creator.

His love is in every bird, animal, flower, bud, river,
greenfield, shrub and tree.
The moon, stars, sunshine, rain, wind, snow, cloud,
and every creature of the sea.

He has given them to us as an expression of His love,
as His desire is to make us happy.
We are surrounded by God, He wraps us in His love,
even though Him we cannot see.

Let the beauty and sweetness of the earth fill our
hearts with joy and delight.
We are close to God as He speaks to us through what
He has made - a breath-taking sight.

Linda Roberts

God's Creation

When we plant a tiny seed
We never know what it will yield
Will it grow or fade away
Or bloom with beauty some-day
There it lies beneath the ground
Until spring comes around.

A garden is a beautiful thing
Daffodils herald the coming of spring
Tiny snow-drops and tulips tall
All this beauty God made them all
He sent the sunshine and the showers
To cultivate these lovely flowers.

There's peace and love in a garden
And you will find it there too
If you take a stroll at eventide
To admire the beautiful view
Gods presence is found everywhere
Even on the scented air.

Gods creation is a wonderful thing
It makes your heart want to sing
No other artist could have painted such scenes
Of country-side and mountain streams
To give such beauty to me and you
This is Gods love in a scenic view.

H M Regan

God's World

How beautiful is Gods world,
the sea the sky the land,
the trees the earth.
        A gift from God to enjoy,
        to replenish it we must.
It can be beautiful again,
but only if we really try.
        It has become so polluted
        so sad.
Can we manage it before
we die.
        If we don't who will
        will it be you?
Can it become whole again,
a world of beauty
as it once was.
        Why did we have to spoil it,
        reduce it to its former glory.
It can be done,
if we really want to.
        It will take time,
        but that is what we have,
        as long as we use it wisely.
How much time though,
only God has the answer.
        We must hope he will grant us
        enough time.
It is up to you!

Brenda Russell

Beautiful Garden

Beautiful garden -God gave you life,
Breathing colour into your dull veins,
Watching you grow strong and proud.
Beautiful garden - so grateful am I,
You chose to flourish here with me,
I can see all of nature welcomes you.

Crowned with jewels in the autumn morning mist;
Greeted by friends on delicate, patterned wings;
Visited by sweet toothed folk buzzing with excitement;
Worshipped by the sun on glorious summer days;
Shrouded by raindrops during April afternoons;
Protected by earth in frosty winter months.

Beautiful garden -
thankyou for these moments.

Dawn Harwood

Snow Drops A Legend

Silence fell upon the garden,
The blossomed trees, the calling birds,
Whirring, humming, shimmering, singing,
Lemur, lyre-bird, tiny gold crest,
Panther, leopard, sprawling lioness,
Spotted deer and muted swan,
Sleek-coat otter, flying fruit bat,
Angled cedar, mossed by green,
Stippled sunlight, ferns great fronded,
Bell hung petals sought by bees,
Drowsy, warm and velvet padded,
Hung with silence and disgrace.

Angel with a flaming sword.

Down in woodlands, tangled, troubled,
Torn by thorns and clutched by briars,
Eve and Adam found no refuge,
No shelter from the knifing cold,
Eye-lids red with beating ice-wind,
Hoar trees hostile, frozen streams,
Grief companion, twisted terror,
Sobbing sorrow, frightened mind.
Caught the passing flight of angels,
Caught the youngest and most kind.
Folded wings and hands of healing,
Small kind hands to combat grief,
Consolation, fire of spirit,
Dazzling, haloed, smiling,
Brief.

As they peered through outspread fingers,
At the 'lumined fading light,
All the tears they'd shed through woodlands
Turned in joy to shining white,
Crystal vistas, frozen beauty,
Triple-petalled, undefiled,
Green-speared, humble,
Perfect herald,
Drops of snow,
Left by a child.

Rosalind Taylor

When God Created Woman

God strolled in his beautiful garden,
the nurtured splendour of love everlasting.
Creation comes with pure thought;
to create woman is what he sought.

Flowers swaying as they danced in the breeze,
a scarlet beauty caught the Lord's glance.
Touching the soft, perfect petals,
the Lord knelt upon his knees.

Soft velvet, filled with grace,
God created woman's loving face.
The joy he felt became her heart,
for joy gives strength with which to start.

Streaming rays of hope
shined down upon her velvet shoulders.
Woman's belief in all of life,
shall be the key to help other's cope.

Exquisite song of the Nightingale,
the Lord decided woman's voice shall be heard.
With gentle notes she will carry,
the wisdom in song, and God's loving word.

Like the beautiful velvet rose,
a woman with pride shall flourish.
Belief in her capabilities and freedom of choice,
will be emulated in her request, of your voice.

Patricia M Kenyon

The Wedding

See the church is filling slowly,
With the friends from far and near,
Here we see the dear relations,
Young and older gathered here.

Now we hear the voices calling -
Greeting friends old and new,
Dressed in many lovely colours,
Palest shades to deeper hues.

Look around and see the flowers,
Chosen with great love and care,
Yellow roses, cream carnations,
Mixed with foliage green and fair.

Now the church is quietly waiting,
For the bride to arrive,
As she comes through the doorway -
The Trumpet Voluntary's played.

As the ceremony commences,
And the hymns are sung,
Then the solemn dedication,
Echoes through the highest beams.

As the bride and bridegroom
Quietly make their vows,
Loving looks and rings exchanged,
On this their glorious day of days.

We hear a wonderful address
Then a hymn sung with zest,
Now the register is signed,
Smiles and good wishes abound.

As the happy pair emerge,
Expectation in the air -
For you see just outside
A red Ferrari in which they ride!

What a truly great occasion.
It has been for all to share
Dear Jonathan and Libby -
'Gods Blessing' to a lovely pair.

Cordelia D Adams

Reason For Living

Over and over and over again,
The thought comes into my mind,
What is the reason for living,
And who was it created mankind.
    Some people believe that man has evolved,
    From the day that the world first began,
    And others believe that there is a God,
    And it was He who has created man.
But it may well be that both are correct,
And that man has gradually evolved,
But that God has always been present,
And that He was always involved.
    But if we were created by God,
    Or if we just happen to be,
    There must be a right way of living,
    If we are to fulfil our destiny.
Well I believe that there is a God,
Who reigns up in Heaven above,
And He has given us a reason for living,
And that reason for living is love.
    Love that we can show to each other,
    And the friendship with others we share,
    The thought and the time that we can give,
    To show that we really do care.
If we can start to fulfil this purpose,
Which is part of the eternal plan,
We shall show that there is a reason,
Why God first created man.
    The reason that man should live in harmony,
    With God and His fellow man,
    What a pity that so very few people,
    Have ever heard of the plan.

R Martin

God

Generator of
life.
Thou art worship due.
The sacredness of
living things
comes from You.
They spring from your
bosom -
to be
protected and nourished.
Anything else
is subordinate
to this.
Why
have givers of laws
not grasped this?

P OFE

Our Miracle

Thank you my darling husband
For our beautiful baby son
He's warm and soft with big blue eyes
He's going to be such fun
It looks as if he's got your shaped ears
Maybe your dimpled cheeks
I can't believe he's here at last
I can't stop taking peeps.

I'm restless now, I'm longing to see your face
I want to place him in your arms
In his shawl of silk and lace
The look of love, the pride, the joy,
When I present you my love, with our son, our boy.

Lilian Roundhill

Before The Time Of Greed

Oak and Ash, Beech and Elm,
part of God's created realm.
Bluebells, Cowslips and Primrose so yellow,
Hedges with Snowdrops, Poppies in meadow.
Badgers, Foxes, Harvest Mice, Mole,
Polecats, Otters and Water Vole,
Osprey, Buzzard, Kestrel and Kite,
Tawny and Barn Owl hunting by night.
Craftsman in workshops, horses pulling ploughs,
Mothers home with children, milk from grazing cows.
Streams with tiddlers in water clear.
Music with melody so sweet to hear.
Artists skill showing beauty to please the eye.
Walks in the country with just birds in the sky.
Places of quiet, air fresh and clean,
Streets safe for marbles, great trains of steam.
A shake of the hand meant a man's true bond,
With honour and faith, not fear being conned.
Sport played for fun of just playing the game,
Winning a cap was a players main aim.
-You saw it for real Great Granddad?
  Is that why you're now so sad?'
  'Yes lad I really saw it, switch that thing off and heed,
  it seems so long ago now, when life was real indeed.
  It seems so long ago now, before the time of speed.
  It seems so long ago now, before the time of greed.'

R Bishop

Words Of Jesus

Consider the lilies how they grow
What beauty and wonder we see
God has created a thing so lovely
Can He not do the same for me
Why do I worry over what I should I wear
Scrimping to afford something new
The God who is Lord of creation
Has promised to supply all my needs too
And consider the humble sparrows
Our joy as we watch them feed
They don't have to work from eight to five
God provides for their every need
He clothes them and feeds them through winter's long days
Their song of thanks we've all heard
God's creation who trust Him for everything
Come and go as free as a bird
God created you and me
And promised our needs to supply
It's our faith in Him that is lacking
Growing less . . . the harder we try
To be our own man . . . provide for our needs
When our Father up above
Created the whole wonder of the universe
And says to us in love
Trust Me my child for everything
Your food . . . your health . . . your dress
Consider the lilies the birds of the air
Look at all nature it's yours to possess . . .

Irene Spencer

Memories

Thank you God for a memory
from childhood times come back to me,
of two souls walking in harmony
in the autumn under a golden tree.

Thank you God for showing me
something of Your presence to see,
in the autumn under a red gold tree
two souls walking, in loves harmony.

Jessica Davies

The Eve Of Creation

God said,
'Let there be light'.
So it was,
Followed by night.
Sunbeams danced,
Stardust swirled
Night slept,
As day unfurled.
Oceans swarmed,
The Earth knew life
Then came Adam,
And from his rib, a wife,
Unashamedly Naked
They became as one
The Eve of Creation
The Race had begun

Jeanette Latta

Precious Moments

A Glimpse of heaven in a rainbow
A sunset moment we can share
The first cry of a baby
The cherished words 'I Care'
The moment when your wish comes true
When you doubted far too long
The pleasure of a friendship
The joy of love in a song
The sudden song of a skylark
As it rises up so high
The soothing sound the river makes
As it goes gurgling by
The caressing warmth of the summer sun
That strokes you into sleep
The fleeting glimpse of a butterfly
That's too beautiful to keep
The tender touch of a loved one
As you hold each other hand
What more can life envisage
We know that all was planned
How can we then not marvel
At all things great and small
The cricket and the grasshopper
The trees so strong and tall
These all are precious moments
We live with and enjoy
Each with its special message
Of beauty that does not cloy. . .

Vera M Coote

The Wonder Of You

You are the day, You are the night
You are the darkness, You are the light.
You are the leaf, You are the tree
You are the ocean, You are the sea,
You are everywhere we go.
You are the rain, You are the snow
You are the one who helps us so
You give us strength when we are low
You are know to many by a different name
But all your works are the same
You are the smile on a child's face
Whatever their colour, religion or race
You are the creator the God above
You are everything. You are love

Robert Beach

Creation

'Everything in creation is symmetrical'
said the Christmas Lecturer at Royal Institution;
earlier, on TV, Hawkins revealed the mystery -
the man unable to walk, who barely can speak,
with the mind of infinite power -
'We shall discover the source and content of the universe
but to understand why, we must enter the mind of God'.

The rooted Chestnut on Kew Green
opens a myriad wings bearing candles of spring;
the air is sweet with perfume of rainbow flowers
and fountains of birdsong rise and refresh our souls.
All through our year, even when earth seems sleeping,
the mighty oceans cleanse the waiting shores,
while stars are sailing the skies.

Creation is never ceasing,
not in six days or the innumerable aeons
light years before and after . . .
                                        But,
as Yeats well knew,
the universe also is in the blade of grass
in our own back garden.

Jean de Leon Mason

February Refugees

I am a February refugee
still hurting from the chilling heat of war
which saw our homes destroyed and made us flee
and left us nothing as it was before . . .

I am a February refugee
rejoicing in the healing balm of spring
with all its precious grace and greenery
which leads me back to my Redeemer King!

Manfred Reuser

The Bluebell Wood

Bang! Bang! Click!
The car is locked.
Assaults of noise and colour stop;
just stillness.
Subtle sounds and shapes
caress our battered nerves,
the trees enfold us like a lover's arms
as we pad softly in.
The world is upside down;
the sky beneath our feet star-studded blue,
light green floats overhead.
I feel myself change gear.

In winter months this place has been
barren and brown;
bare fingers reaching up as if
entreating spring to come.
What was so dull and dead,
clammy and cold,
silent and still,
is pulsing now with life.

Perfume and song pervade the air.
The bees buzz gently flower to flower.
Fat buds are bursting on the trees
with folded furry fans expanding
clothing twigs with feather-lace.
A myriad floral bells are ringing
and I find my heart is singing
with all nature praising God.

Wendy Allen

A Moment Of Magic

I walked the beach this morning
Sometimes stumbling in my step
Selecting shells and stubbing a stone
Savouring just this time alone.

Slowly, I became aware
Of somewhere out of vision
Where something surely had caught my eye
Though nothing now could I espy.

Just then from the depths of nowhere
A majestic beauty rose
Grey body wet with seductive sheen
A Dolphin - an oceanic queen.

She swam with such intention
Unaware her distance from shore
I prayed God, without a sound,
Stop her, please, from coming aground!

Without a glance she slipped away
Leaving to me this magic day.

Connie Huntingdon

Swallow

Fly with the wind swift swallow
impressed on a clear blue sky.
Soar with the surf dear swallow
as ships go sailing by.
Reach for the stars sweet swallow
as sun-rise peeps its eye.
Glide with the clouds weary swallow
the end of time is nigh
Fall to the earth brave swallow
your breast stung with a shot
Limp on the ground my swallow
white on scarlet left to rot
Though I will remember you gliding
swooping to the seas
Spirit of a swallow floating on
the breeze.

Inga Hass

Reflecting On A Drive Through The Trough Of Bowland

Where bluebells grow
Banks of green
Deep ravine
Streams below
Hungry hue
For my soul.

Heavenly blue
Periwinkle too
Eye and sea and sky
Blue
I love you

Elizabeth Leslie

Awakenings

Spring
Sun
Blue skies
Robins
Budding Green Trees
Butterflies
Flowers
Imagination
New dreams

Colin Zarhett

Tinitis Blues

It began in my beginning time early,
Sitting with my Mum in our pew.
The chapel preacher hell-fired most clearly,
Impassioned with the man he called Duw.

All round and about and within me,
Were the tenets to uplift our kind.
But all was not as it should be,
When part deafness crept into my mind.

Young was I then, odds twenty,
Journalled barely to scrip.
Much was there to write and plenty,
With youth's term most eager for script.

But I was forlorn of essay,
Unhappy of spirit and will.
Religions words were a hearsay,
Text written of an old fashioned quill.

Reclused I not to an outcast,
Each day taxed labour with deed.
But day's gone found that at repast,
I sought not to socialise need.

Inward thoughts turned to humility,
Where the white coats use scalpel and dope.
When within wards I saw the futility,
Of those bed bound in frailty, sans hope.

No more at my beginnings time station,
Train whistling ear blasts continue;
I journey on to my next destination,
O? The guard on my train? He's called Duw!

Elwyn Johnson

Birth Of Janice

A new life now has just begun
With many a thrill and joy to say
The child shines there like morning sun
Rising above all at break of day

Like a budding rose there she lies
And will grow rich in all her bloom
Stirring now and then with cries
Enchanting all within the room

At ten-past midnight last Thursday morn
This little angel did appear
So neat and perfect in all her form
Filling our hearts with joy and cheer

So from now on I'm sure she'll be
Treated with love in the best of ways
And grow from this 'Little Lass' we see
To the 'Lass' she'll be in later days

William D H Cook